THE ELIZABETHANS

THE ELIZABETHANS

INTRODUCED

BY

ALLARDYCE NICOLL

CAMBRIDGE

AT THE UNIVERSITY PRESS

1957

PUBLISHED BY
THE SYNDICS OF THE CAMBRIDGE UNIVERSITY PRESS
London Office: Bentley House, N.W.1
American Branch: New York
Agents for Canada, India, and Pakistan: Macmillan

Printed in Great Britain at the University Press, Cambridge
(Brooke Crutchley, University Printer)

CONTENTS

v

PREFACE

In this book an attempt is made to allow the Elizabethans to give an image of their times in their own words and in their own pictures. Pictures and words are regarded here as of equal importance, and consequently the former have been incorporated in the text, not relegated to separate plates as supplementary material. Since, in general, choice has been made of pictorial material which tells its own story, captions have deliberately been omitted; references to the subjects and sources appear in the Notes.

Obviously, an anthology such as this can hope to do no more than provide a general glimpse of the time. Peculiarly idiosyncratic expressions of belief have been avoided and selection has been made of extracts which, while all of them bear the stamp of their authors' personalities, might be paralleled by others of similar content. In the selection, preference has been given to those passages which seemed most trenchantly to put forward a point of view or statement of fact and to those which aided me in my endeavour to provide a logical development of theme—for, although the extracts are from many sources and mingle verse and prose, I have sought, where possible, to make one extract lead on to another. With this object in view, I have occasionally introduced very short quotations, even single sentences, as links between others of greater length.

Most of these quotations come strictly within the span of Elizabeth's reign, although a few have been admitted from before 1558 and a few from the years immediately following 1603, where the authors had succeeded in expressing with peculiar force observations or ideas which as readily might have belonged to this period. Naturally, numerous paragraphs have had to be taken from the works of such well-known recorders as William Harrison and Fynes Moryson, but otherwise I have endeavoured to present accounts from as varied an array of contemporary writers as possible.

Since we are not concerned here with authors' texts, the extracts have been modernized in spelling and punctuation. There might have been a value in exemplifying the diversity of spelling and pointing to be found in this age, but the sudden moving from one writer's practice to another's would clearly have destroyed the attempt to make the quotations flow easily one to another and so form a consistent whole. On the other hand, as the Notes will indicate, almost all the extracts are taken from original, not from edited, versions. While due care has been exercised to ensure faithfulness to these originals, I have permitted myself to introduce certain clearly necessary emendations, to omit phrases, and even sentences, without the use of the dots commonly employed to mark elisions, to leave out speakers' names in extracts from plays, substituting generic titles for specifically named characters, and (in two passages) to insert proper nouns, derived from preceding paragraphs in the originals, for the pronouns which actually appeared in the passages quoted.

In a book, of the same length as this, written by a modern historian on the subject of life in Elizabethan England, no doubt it would have been possible to present many more details and to touch on more varied aspects of the common life of the time; yet there seems to me to be a special value in letting the story of the Elizabethan age thus take shape in the language, poetic and prose, of its own people. Perhaps in this way there is less danger of obscuring or colouring the facts and concepts by the intrusion of modern comments inevitably conditioned by an idea of the universe, of the state and of man which would have been incomprehensible to men of the sixteenth century.

I wish to express my sincere thanks to the many owners of pictures here reproduced for their permissions so courteously given: full acknowledgments are given in the Notes. I wish, also, to thank Professor Ellis Waterhouse for his advice and assistance and Mr R. F. Hill for his kindness in checking some of the extracts.

A. N.

THE SHAKESPEARE INSTITUTE
(UNIVERSITY OF BIRMINGHAM)
STRATFORD-UPON-AVON

August 1956

The Paradox

INCONSISTENCY rules in human affairs, but the measure of inconsistency varies from age to age. Some periods of civilization cloak better than others diversity in opinion and in practice; in some the inconsistencies are largely unconsidered by contemporaries, in others they become fully conscious and the subject of anxious debate. It is precisely such extensive inconsistency which may be taken as a prime symbol of the Elizabethan age. Conflicts, contraries, dominate in thought and in action, leading towards confusion in several spheres of mental and practical activity but also inducing resolutions whence springs the true power of the time. If we seek for the inner core of Shakespeare's strength, we shall find it, perhaps, after all our search, in the paradox and in the enigma; and in this Shakespeare was but giving profound expression to the mood of his compatriots. The contrast of light and darkness, of good and evil, has rarely been so potent or so potently exemplified in literature. Hardly any other age has been so oppressed by the ominous awareness of Death's fell scythe or so replete with the sheer joy of living. We are in the presence here of extremes—a brilliance that scintillates the more radiantly because of surrounding shadows, an exuberance that intoxicates more intensely because of a prevailing melancholy.

Look where we will, from the Queen down to the humblest of her subjects, from the age's apparel to the achievements of its poets, this will seem to be the key cut best to unlock its secrets.

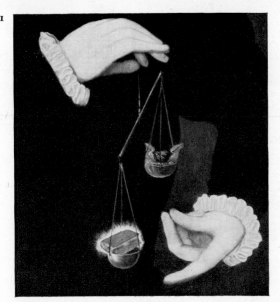

The most cunning and curious music is that which is made out of discords.

Can *discord* then (so much dispraisèd) be
    The mean to keep things by their *contraries*?
Can *enmity* have such equal degree
    As may make *union* in *qualities*?
    Hath sad *contention* such sweet faculties
As may support in true tranquillity
The bodies wherein is *disunity*?

Nothing appears, or can be said the thing,
    Without the contrary: *dark* from the *light*,
Sickness from *health*, cold *winter* from the *spring*,
    True *peace* from *war*, sweet *love* from foul
        despite,
    Just from *unjust*, *truth* from the thing *unright*,
None can distinguish but by *qualities*
That are discover'd by their *contraries*.

Queen Elizabeth

I T is appropriate that the queen of this age should herself have been an enigma. Graced with all the feminine foibles, vain, pleasure-loving, rejoicing in rich attire and the sparkle of jewels, she yet displayed all the masculine virtues. Refusing to marry, she created a court of lovers. Unpredictable and the despair of counsellors who sought to fathom her intentions, she was now all gentleness, now high imperious as though she were the image of Henry VIII wrapped in virginity.

The flatteries she countenanced seem at times so fulsome as to become ridiculous, but paradoxically they savoured of truth. Her successor, James, also demanded adulation; but the private and often indiscreet comments of later courtiers can find no parallel in her reign. Even those who were not of her palace circle were caught up in the prevailing atmosphere. A foreign visitor to her court saw on the throne an old woman with a hooked nose and blackened teeth, her cheeks artificially rouged and her auburn tresses obviously false; but to him she 'appeared like a goddess such as painters are wont to depict'.

Moving from place to place in her progresses, she sought and demanded the most glorious of entertainment, yet she was eager to accept with thanks purses

3

containing a paltry few sovereigns. With consummate political adroitness she made England play a mighty part on the confused and dangerous international scene, yet her parsimony was notorious, her army was maintained under strictest economy and her navy was upheld rather by private enterprise than at the expense of the state.

A woman who firmly held the reins of authority in her long slender fingers, she found time to make and to keep herself one of the most accomplished princely scholars of her age. Even if we allow for some exaggeration, we are forced to admire her intellectual pursuits. A wide and constant reader in many languages, she could turn at will from the modern tongues to the ancient. More afraid of making an error in her latinity than of any prince in Christendom, she could, in her old age, berate an impertinent Polish envoy in an impromptu Latin oration which left him and her courtiers in word-bereft amazement.

In two things she was utterly constant. Although she might appear at times to be dallying with the thought of marriage, she dared dangerously but successfully to defy all public opinion and keep herself a maiden queen. She wanted no husband; her husbands were her people—for, in the end, the true secret of her power is seen to lie in the sincere and enduring love she ever expressed for her subjects, a love which, even when men were most puzzled and dismayed by her actions, was returned a thousandfold.

4

5 Are you then travelling to the temple of Eliza?

'Even to her temple are my feeble limbs travelling. Some call her Pandora, some Gloriana, some Cynthia, some Belphoebe, some Astraea—all by several names to express several loves. Yet all those names make but one celestial body, as all those loves meet to create but one soul.'

I am one of her own country, and we adore her by the name of Eliza.

We were admitted into the presence-chamber, 6 hung with rich tapestry, and the floor, after the English fashion, strewed with hay, through which the Queen commonly passes in her way to chapel. At the door stood a gentleman dressed in velvet, with a gold chain, whose office was to introduce to the Queen any person of distinction that came to wait on her. It was Sunday, when there is usually the greatest attendance of nobility. In the same hall were the Archbishop of Canterbury, the Bishop of London, a great number of counsellors of state, officers of the crown and gentlemen, who waited the Queen's coming out; which she did from her own apartment when it was time to go to prayers, attended in the following manner:

First went gentlemen, barons, earls, knights of the Garter, all richly dressed and bareheaded; next came the Lord High Chancellor of England, bearing the seals in a red-silk purse, between two, one of whom carried the royal sceptre, the other the sword of state in a red scabbard studded with golden fleurs-de-lis, the

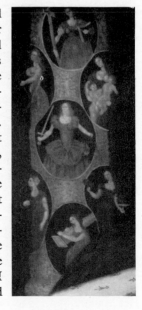

point upwards. Next came the Queen, in the sixty-fifth year of her age as we were told, very majestic; her face oblong, fair, but wrinkled; her eyes small, yet black and pleasant; her nose a little hooked; her lips narrow, and her teeth black (a defect the English seem subject to, from their too great use of sugar). She had in her ears two pearls, with very rich drops. Her hair was of an auburn colour, but false; upon her head she had a small crown. Her bosom was uncovered, as all the English ladies have it till they marry, and she had on a necklace of exceeding fine jewels. Her hands were slender, her fingers rather long, and her stature neither tall nor low. Her air was stately, her manner of speaking mild and obliging. That day she was dressed in white silk, bordered with pearls of the size of beans, and over it a mantle of black silk shot with silver threads; her train was very long, the end of it borne by a marchioness; instead of a chain, she had an oblong collar of gold and jewels.

The ladies of the court followed next to her, very handsome and well-shaped, and for the most part dressed in white. She was guarded on each side by the gentlemen pensioners, fifty in number, with gilt halberds. In the ante-chapel next the hall where we were, petitions were presented to her, and she received them most graciously, which occasioned the acclamation of 'God save the Queen Elizabeth!' She answered it with, 'I thank you, mine good people'.

By Sir Christopher Hatton: a collar of gold.
By the Earl of Shrewsbury: in gold, £20.
By the Earl of Sussex: in gold, £10.
By the Earl of Ormonde: part of a petticoat of carnation satin.
By the Countess of Lincoln: a long cloak of murrey velvet.
By the Countess of Pembroke: in gold, £10.
By the Countess of Ormonde: part of a petticoat of carnation satin.
By the Countess of Bath: a fan of swan down.
By the Archbishop of Canterbury: in gold, £40.
By the Bishop of London: in gold, £20.
By the Bishop of Lichfield and Coventry: in gold and silver, £13. 6s. 8d.
By the Lord Hunsdon, Lord Chamberlain: the nether skirts of the covering of a gown.
By Sir Francis Walsingham, Principal Secretary: a cloak and safeguard of fair coloured velvet.
By Sir Thomas Layton, Captain of Guernsey: a petticoat of white sarcenet.
By Sir Robert Sidney: a doublet of white satin.

10   'I do assure you that there is no prince that loveth his subjects better, or whose love can countervail our love; there is no jewel, be it of never so rich a prize, which I prefer before this jewel; I mean your love, for I do more esteem it than any treasure or riches—for that we know how to prize, but love and thanks I count inestimable. And though God hath raised me high, yet this I count the glory of my crown—that I have reigned with your loves. This makes me that I do not so much rejoice that God hath made me to be a queen, as to be a queen over so thankful a people.'

11   Robert Phillips, Bailiff, rising out of the place where he kneeled, approached now to the coach or chariot wherein Her Majesty sat, and, coming to the side thereof, kneeling down offered unto Her Majesty a purse very fair wrought and in the purse twenty pounds all in sovereigns, which Her Majesty, putting forth her hand, received—showing withal a very beaming and gracious countenance.

By Sir Thomas Cecil: a French gown of black silk network.

By Mr Skidamour: part of a loose gown of black taffeta.

By Mr Doctor Lopus: a pair of perfumed gloves.

15   On Sunday my lord of London preached to the Queen's Majesty and seemed to touch on the vanity of decking the body too finely. Her Majesty told the ladies that 'if the bishop held more discourse on such matters, she would fit him for Heaven—but he should walk thither without a staff and leave his mantle behind him'. Perchance the bishop hath never sought Her Highness' wardrobe, or he would have chosen another text.

Her mind was oft-time like the gentle air that 17 cometh from the westerly point in a summer's morn; 'twas sweet and refreshing to all around her. Her speech did win all affections, and her subjects did try to shew all love to her commands; for she would say, 'her state did require her to command what she knew her people would willingly do from their own love to her'. Herein did she shew her wisdom fully; for who did choose to lose her confidence, or who would withhold a shew of love and obedience, when their Sovereign said it was their own choice, and not her compulsion? Surely she did play well her tables to gain obedience thus without constraint: again, she could put forth such alterations, when obedience was lacking, as left no doubtings whose daughter she was.

16   'I thank God I am endued with such qualities that, if I were turned out of the realm in my petticoat, I were able to live in any place in Christendom.'

soothe with great semblance of good liking to all around, and cause every one to open his most inward thought to her; when, on a sudden, she would ponder in private on what had passed, write down all their opinions, draw them out as occasion required, and sometime disprove to their faces what had been delivered a month before. Hence she knew every one's part, and by thus *fishing*, as Hatton said, she caught many poor fish who little knew what snare was laid for them.

As I did bear so much love toward Her Majesty, I know not well how to stop my tales of her virtues, and sometimes her faults, for *nemo nascitur sine*—saith the poet; but even her errors did seem great marks of surprising endowments. When she smiled, it was a pure sunshine, that every one did choose to bask in, if they could; but anon came a storm from a sudden gathering of clouds, and the thunder fell in wondrous manner on all alike. I never did find greater show of understanding and learning than she was blest with; and whoever liveth longer than I can will look back and become *laudator temporis acti*.

21 Her Highness was wont to soothe her ruffled temper with reading every morning, when she had been stirred to passion at the council, or other matters had overthrown her gracious disposition. She did much admire Seneca's wholesome advisings, when the soul's quiet was flown away; and I saw much of her translating thereof. By art and nature together so blended, it was difficult to find her right humour at any time. Her wisest men and best counsellors were oft sore troubled to know her will in matters of state; so covertly did she pass her judgment as seemed to leave all to their discreet management; and, when the business did turn to better advantage, she did most cunningly commit the good issue to her own honour and understanding; but, when ought fell out contrary to her will and intent, the Council were in great straight to defend their own acting and not blemish the Queen's good judgment.

Sir Christopher Hatton was wont to say: 'The Queen did fish for men's souls, and had so sweet a bait, that no one could escape her network.' In truth, I am sure her speech was such as none could refuse to take delight in, when frowardness did not stand in the way. I have seen her smile,

For this Lady, though not prophetically yet, 22 like a provident princess, in the series of things and times, foresaw, through the long-lasting wisdom of government, a quintessence, howsoever abstracted out of moral philosophy and human laws, yet many degrees in use of mankind above them. She, I say, foresaw that every excess of passion expressed from the monarch in acts or counsels of estate would infallibly stir up in the people the like cobwebs of a popular spinning, and therefore from these piercing grounds she concluded that a steady hand in the government of sovereignty would ever prove more prosperous than any nimble or witty practice, crafty shifting or imperious forcing humours possibly could do.

With the same caution in all her doings she made merit precious, honour dainty and her graces passing rare, keeping them (as the Venetians do their curiously refined gold) to set an edge upon the industry of man, and yet (like branches of creation) sparingly reserved within

the circuit of her throne, as inherent and tender prerogatives not fit to be left at random in the power of ambitious favourites or low-looking counsellors, whose ends are seldom so large or safe for the public as the native prince's counsels are, or ought to be.

During her life, what peace in her country! what plenty in her land! what triumphs in her court! what learning in her schools! what trades in her cities! what wealth in her kingdom! what wisdom in her counsel and what grace in her government! Who durst to annoy her but the enemies of God's word, who felt the hand of His wrath for seeking the hurt of His anointed? Whom held she her friends but the favourers of God's truth, and to whom was she an enemy but to the enemies of the same? What monarch ever sent to her whose ambassador did not admire her, and what prince did ever hear of her who did not worthily honour her? Was she not mistress of the narrow seas and feared even in the ocean? Did not the heathen know her power and Christians sue for her favour? O let me speak of her majesty but with admiration whom God had blessed with so much perfection! Was not the soldier rewarded, the scholar cherished, the lawyer advanced, the merchant enriched and the tradesman maintained? Yea, had not the rich their pleasure and the poor their relief, the stranger pity and the subject peace—and all under the hand of God, in the eye of her grace and care of her government—and can all this be forgotten? Did not her trumpets sound rather passa measures than points of war, and her drums rather beat dances than warlike marches, and her horses not rather neigh in the pride of their furniture than in fury against the enemy? Was not music in her best key in her court, and what art was excellent in her kingdom that had not grace in her favour? What state in more majesty, what court in more state, what counsel in more honour, and what honour in more grace?

25

Both in her life and her death she was ap- 26 pointed to be the mirror of her time.

12

The Spheres of Heaven and Earth

THE STARS ABOVE US

No understanding of the Elizabethan age is possible without a full and complete recognition of the fact that for these men the proper study of mankind was God. The universe for them was at once mysterious and relatively simple. Not being worried by inconsistencies, the seamen might chart their courses as though the earth were flat, and even those who knew of the theories of Copernicus could easily assimilate the new into the old system—and this system was the Ptolemaic pattern of concentric spheres, conceived as having the earth's globe immovable in its centre. Poets and scientists alike bowed to its authority.

Everyone, too, believed that from the stars strange influences flowed down upon the terrestrial realm. In vain do we search in this age for any clear and emphatic denial of stellar or planetary power. Some advanced thinkers might question whether the scope of such powers could come within the orbit of human wisdom; many others might ridicule the claims of common astrological quacks and of quacks, like John Dee and Simon Forman, who were not so common; but all acknowledged that, in one way or another, man's life was conditioned by forces emanating from the spheres or by God's will working through them. The sole declarations of complete denial of this truth are those put by dramatists on the lips of characters evil in their reliance on self—characters ultimately brought crashing to their deserved ruin.

27 Generally the most part of the seamen make their account as though the earth were a platform.

28   Some also deny that the Earth is in the middest of the world, and some affirm that it is moveable, as also Copernicus—by way of supposition, and not for that he thought so indeed—who affirmeth that the Earth turneth about and that the Sun standeth still in the midst of the heavens; by help of which false supposition he hath made truer demonstrations of the motions and revolutions of the celestial spheres than ever were made before, as plainly appeareth by his book *De revolutionibus*, dedicated to Paulus Tertius the Pope in the year of our Lord 1536. But Ptolemy, Aristotle and all other old writers affirm the Earth to be in the middest, and to remain unmoveable and to be in the very centre of the world, proving the same with many most strong reasons not needful here to be rehearsed, because I think few or none do doubt thereof, and specially the Holy Scripture affirming the foundations of the Earth to be laid so sure that it never should move at any time.

29   How prove you the frame of the world to be round?

'By three reasons. First, by comparison, for the likeness which it hath with the chief idea or shape of God's mind, which hath neither beginning nor ending, and therefore is compared to a circle. Secondly, by aptness as well of moving as of containing; for, if it were not round of shape, it should not be so apt to turn about as it continually doth, nor to contain so much as it doth, for the round figure is of greatest capacity and containeth most. Thirdly, necessity proveth it to be round; for, if it were with angles or corners, it should not be so apt to turn about, and, in turning about, it should leave void and empty places, which nature abhorreth.'

Whereupon is this sphere or great round frame turned?

'Upon two most firm and immoveable hooks, called in Latin *cardines mundi* and in Greek *poli*.'

What doth the celestial part contain?

'The eleven Heavens and Spheres. In ascending orderly upwards from the elements they be these. The first is the sphere of the Moon; the second, the sphere of Mercury; the third, the sphere of Venus; the fourth, the sphere of the Sun; the fifth, the sphere of Mars; the sixth, the sphere of Jupiter; the seventh, the sphere of Saturn; the eighth, the sphere of the Fixed Stars, commonly called the Firmament; the ninth is called the Second Moveable or Crystal Heaven; the tenth is called the First Moveable; and the eleventh is called the Imperial Heaven, where God and his angels are said to dwell.

The Imperial Heaven, as our ancient divines affirm, is unmoveable, and this Heaven, being the foundation of the world, is most fine and pure in substance, most round of shape, most great in quantity, most clear in quality and most high in place.

The tenth sphere or Heaven, called in Latin *primum mobile*, is also of a most pure and clear substance, and without stars; and it continually moveth with an equal gate from East to West, making his revolution in twenty-four hours.

The ninth Heaven is also clear of substance, and without stars, having two movings, the one from east to west upon the poles of the world, according to the daily moving of the First Moveable, and the other from west to east upon his own poles, according to the succession of the signs of the Zodiac, which is in the First Moveable, turning so slowly about as it maketh but one degree in a hundred years.

The eighth Heaven, otherwise called the Firmament, is a most glorious Heaven adorned with all the Fixed Stars, called Fixed because they are fastened in this Heaven like knots in a knotty board, having no moving of themselves, but are moved according to the moving of this eighth sphere or Heaven wherein they are fixed.'

30   The stars be of the same substance that the Heavens are wherein they are placed, differing only from the same in thickness; and therefore some, defining a star, do say that it is a bright and shining body and the thickest part of his Heaven, apt both to receive and to retain the light of the Sun and thereby is visible and object to the sight; for the Heaven itself, being most pure, thin, transparent and without colour, is not visible.

31

THE COS-
MOGRAPHI-
cal Glasse, conteinyng
the pleasant Principles
of Cosmographie, Geogra-
phie, Hydrographie,
or Nauigation.

Compiled by VVilliam
Cuningham Doctor
in Physicke.

Excussum Londini in officina
Ioan.Daij Typographi.
Anno.1559.

In this Glasse if you will beholde
The Sterry Skie, and Yearth so wide,
The Seas also, with windes so colde,
Yea and thy selfe all these to guide:
What this Type meane first learne a right,
So shall thy gayne thy travaill quight.

Or for some brawl, which in that chamber high
  They should still dance to please a gazer's
    sight;
For me I do Nature unidle know,
  And know great causes great effects procure,
And know those bodies high reign on the low.

Our lives' effects and fortunes are 35
As is that happy or unlucky star
Which, reigning in our frail nativity,
Seals up the secrets of our destiny,
With friendly planets in conjunction set
Or else with others merely opposite.

36 Astrology is an art mathematical, which reasonably demonstrateth the operations and effects of the natural beams of light and secret influence of the stars and planets in every element and elemental body at all times in any horizon assigned.

37 Certainly it cannot be doubted but the stars are instruments of far greater use than to give an obscure light and for men to gaze on after sunset, it being manifest that the diversity of seasons, the winters and summers more hot and cold, are not so uncertained by the Sun and Moon alone, who always keep one and the same course, but that the stars have also their working therein.

And if we cannot deny but that God hath given virtues to springs and fountains, to cold earth, to plants and stones, minerals and to the excremental parts of the basest living creatures, why should we rob the beautiful stars of their working powers? For, seeing they are many in number, and of eminent beauty and magnitude, we may not think that in the treasury of His wisdom, who is infinite, there can be wanting, even for every star, a peculiar virtue and operation, as every herb, plant, fruit and flower adorning the face of the earth hath the like. For as these were not created to beautify the earth alone, and to cover and shadow her dusty face, but otherwise for the use of man and beast, to feed them and cure them; so were not those uncountable glorious bodies set in the Firmament to no other end than to adorn it, but for instruments and

32 All the Fixed Stars of the Firmament are always of like distance, notwithstanding by reason of the manifold moving of the Firmament wherein they are placed they seem to change their places, for a star, being round of shape, hath no members meet to walk from one place to another, but only changeth his place through the motion of his sphere or Heaven wherein such planet is fixed.

33 But, tell me, hath every sphere a dominion or intelligentia?
  'Ay.'

34 *Though dusky wits dare scorn astrology,*
  And fools can think those lamps of purest
    light—
Whose number, ways, greatness, eternity,
  Promising wonders, wonder do invite—
To have for no cause birthright in the sky
  But for to spangle the black weeds of night,

organs of His divine providence, so far as it hath pleased His just will to determine. Origen upon this place of *Genesis* 'Let there be light in the Firmament, etc.' affirmeth that the stars are not causes (meaning, perchance, binding causes) but are as open books wherein are contained and set down all things whatsoever to come, but not to be read by the eyes of human wisdom: which latter part I believe well. In this question of Fate the middle course is to be followed, that as, with the heathen, we do not bind God to his creatures in this supposed necessity of destiny, so, on the contrary, we do not rob those beautiful creatures of their powers and offices.

Howsoever we are by the stars inclined at our birth, yet there are many things both in nature and art that encounter the same and weaken their operation. There is nothing, after God's reserved power, that so much setteth this art of influence out of square and rule as education doth; for there are none in the world so wickedly inclined but that a religious instruction and bringing-up may fashion anew and reform them, nor any so well disposed whom, the reins being let loose, the continual fellowship and familiarity and the examples of dissolute men may not corrupt and deform.

38

Saturn is an enemy to human nature, a destroyer of life, malevolent, cold, dry, earthly, masculine, of the day, the greater infortune of man's body; he rules the right ear, the spleen, the bladder and the bones; of humours, melancholy mixt with phlegm; of persons, old men, husbandmen, miners, masons, tanners, Jews, envious persons, stubborn, solitary, still, lean, beardless, covetous, gluttons, deceivers; husbandry, fruits of the earth, mines of metals, treasurers, buildings, heritage of the dead, possessions, prison; and hath of colours, black.

Jupiter is the greater fortune of the day, hot and moist, benevolent. He rules, in man's body, the liver, lights and lungs, the ribs, the arteries, the blood, the seed, pulses and the left ear. Of humours, the sanguine. He signifieth bishops, prelates, lawyers, judges; shamefast, gentle and humble, just, honest, true, faithful, liberal, virtuous and religious; governors of cities and rich men; ecclesiastical dignities, religion, justice, honesty, praise. Of colours, blue or citrine.

Mars is the lesser infortunate, masculine, of the night, immoderately hot and dry. Of man's body, he governs the gall, the veins, sinews, stones and the left ear; of humours, the choleric; and, of colours, red. He signifieth, of persons, the warriors, seditious, disdainful, conjurers or conspirers, ireful, thieves, cruel, bold, irreverent, murtherers, captains, chirurgeons, Turks, terrible, violent, careless, workers in fire-works, gunners and founders, war, strife, dissention, tyranny, violence, armory, alchemy, and all things wrought and done by the fire.

Sol is the light and lamp of heaven, and gives life natural to all things. He is an indifferent planet, moderately hot and dry, masculine, of the day, fortunate by aspect but infortunate by corporal conjunction. He rules, of man's body, the brain, the marrow, the joints, the right eye of a man and the left eye of a woman. Of colours, deep yellow or gold colour. He signifieth kings, princes, magistrates, famous persons, desirous of honour and ambitious; also kingdoms, empires, nobility, magnanimity, fortitude, glory, rule, honour.

Venus is the lesser fortune, feminine, of the night, cold and moist, temperate, benevolent. Of man's body, she rules the throat, paps, belly, reins, matrix, loins, fat, spleen and the buttocks. Of humours, phlegm; of colours, green and whitish. She signifies, of persons, the fair-conditioned, the merciful, meek, the fine, pleasant and delightsome, the effeminate, lovers, dancers, banqueters, musicians and poets; also flability, jollity, love, mercy, beauty, gifts of friends and women, marriage, dowry, ornaments, jewels, lust and lechery.

Mercury is convertible, good with the good and bad with the bad, sometime masculine and of the day, sometime feminine and of the night, hot with the hot and cold with the cold, moist with the moist and dry with the dry planets, as he is configured to any. He rules, of man's body, the mouth, the tongue, the thoughts, the memory, the hands and the thighs. He signifieth, of persons, philosophers, scriveners, merchants, painters, devisers of subtleties, crafty, deceitful, wavering, lying, proud and scornful. Also all kind of sciences, buying, selling, contracts, honest studies, divination and curiosity. Of colours, the sky colour or the speckled of many colours.

Luna is naturally cold and moist, of the night, feminine. She is the carrier and deliverer of the influence of all the planets through her orb unto us. She rules the left eye of a man and the right eye of a woman, and, of both, the stomach, the taste, the liver, the belly and the left side. She signifieth noble women, widows, the vulgar sort and those of continual motion—as mariners, messengers, legates and vagabonds. Also all things that abound in moisture, the sea, the rivers, with their ebbs and floods, the study of histories, embassages, navigation, journeying, service, planting, sowing and all water-works. Of humour, the phlegm; of colours, white or silver colour.

All beneath the Orb of the Moon

THE ELEMENTS AND MAN

THE central and ever-abiding thought of God meant that the concepts of the Elizabethans were prevailingly theomorphic. The microcosm, which was man, always was explained in terms of the macrocosm, never the macrocosm in terms of human life. Man was pictured not only as wrought in the image of the Deity, but also as holding an essentially significant position in the universe of God's creation. Inhabiting the Elemental region which extended from the Earth to the Moon, he partook of the corruptibility which all things within that region were forced to share, but his mind, though limited, was not subject to such corruption. In one sense, he might be only the chief among nature's animals, but in another the range of his thoughts and the penetrating power of his imagination made him just less than the angels.

That system of correspondences, together with the inconsistencies amid which the Elizabethans dwelled, can be seen nowhere more potently than in the concept of the elements, coupled with the related humours of man's nature. The elements themselves, fire, air, water and earth, could not be viewed in their purity by man, yet man was compounded of them; and to the elements corresponded the four humours or fluids—choler, air, phlegm and melancholy—which formed his bodily essence. Fluids they might be, but some were described as dry, and the most powerful of all the humours was unnatural melancholy, also called burned melancholy or melancholy adust.

Look where we will in Elizabethan literature or life, we cannot escape reference from man to his humours, from the humours to the elements, from the elements to the upper spheres and so finally to the Imperial or Empyreal Heaven of God.

2-2

41 The parts or regions of the world are two, as the Ethereal and Elementary. The Ethereal region is the higher and upper part of the world, which encloseth the Elementary region. The Elementary region is the nether part of the world, which is contained within the hollow upper face of the Moon's orb and sphere, in which are all corruptible bodies and things harmed by diverse alterations, except the mind of man.

42

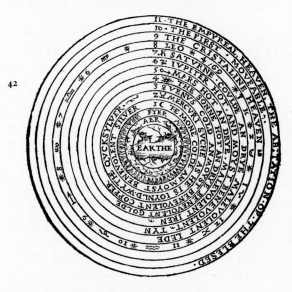

43 Our fleshly frail complexions
Of elemental natures grounded be,
With which our dispositions most agree:
Some of the fire and air participate
And some of watry and of earthy state,
As hot and moist, with chilly cold and dry,
And unto these the other contrary;
And by their influence powerful on the earth
Predominant in man's frail mortal birth.

44 I find by my reading that man was compounded of the four Elements, of Fire, Water, Earth and Air. I thus understand the four Elements— choler, phlegm, blood and melancholy.

45 The purest part, which we call, in comparison and in respect of the rest, *blood*, is temperate in quality and moderate in substance, exceeding all the other parts in quantity if the body be of equal temper, made for nourishment of the most temperate parts and engendering of spirits. The second is *phlegm*, next to blood in quantity, of a watery nature, cold and moist, apt to be converted into the substance of pure blood if nature fail not in her working ordained for nourishment of moister parts. The third is *melancholy*, of substance gross and earthy, cold and dry in regard of the other, in quantity inferior to phlegm, fit nourishment for such parts as are of like temper. The fourth, *choler*, fiery, hot and driest of quality, thin in substance, least in quantity, and ordained for such parts as require subtler nourishment and are tempered with greater portion of the fiery element.

46 Man, thus compounded and formed by God, was an abstract, or model, or brief story of the Universal. Whereas God created three sorts of living natures, to wit, Angelical, Rational and Brutal, giving to Angels an intellectual and to beasts a sensual nature, he vouchsafed unto Man both the intellectual of Angels, the sensitive of Beasts and the proper rational belonging unto Man; and because in the little frame of Man's body there is a representation of the Universal and, by allusion, a kind of participation of all the parts there, therefore was Man called *Microcosmos*, or Little World.

For out of the earth and dust was formed the flesh of man, and therefore heavy and lumpish; the bones of his body we may compare to the hard rocks and stones, and therefore strong and durable. His blood, which disperseth itself by the branches of veins through all the body, may be resembled to those waters which are carried by brooks and rivers over all the earth; his breath to the air; his natural heat to the inclosed warmth which the earth hath in itself, which, stirred up by the heat of the sun, assisteth nature in the speedier procreation of those varieties which the earth bringeth forth. Our radical moisture, oil or balsamum, whereon the natural heat feedeth and is maintained, is resembled to the fat and fertility of the earth; the hairs of man's body, which adorns or overshadows it, to the grass which covereth the upper face and skin of the earth; our generative power, to nature, which produceth all things; our determinations, to the light, wandering and unstable clouds, carried everywhere with uncertain winds; our eyes, to the light of the sun and moon; and the beauty of our youth, to the flowers of the spring, which, either in a very short time or with the sun's heat, dry up and wither away, or the fierce puffs of wind blow them from the stalks; the thoughts of our mind, to the motion of angels, and our pure understanding to those intellectual natures which are always present with God; and, lastly, our immortal souls (while they are righteous) are by God himself beautified with the title of his own image and similitude.

The four complexions resemble the four elements, and the seven ages of man the seven planets, whereof our infancy is compared to the Moon, in which we seem only to live and grow, as plants; the second age to Mercury, wherein we are taught and instructed; our third age to Venus, the days of love, desire and vanity; the fourth to the Sun, the strong, flourishing and beautiful age of man's life; the fifth to Mars, in which we seek honour and victory, and in which our thoughts travail to ambitious ends; the sixth age is ascribed to Jupiter, in which we begin to take account of our times, judge of ourselves and grow to the perfection of our understanding; the last, and seventh, to Saturn, wherein our days are sad and overcast, and in which we find, by dear and lamentable experience and by the loss which can never be repaired, that of all our vain passions and affections past the sorrow only abideth.

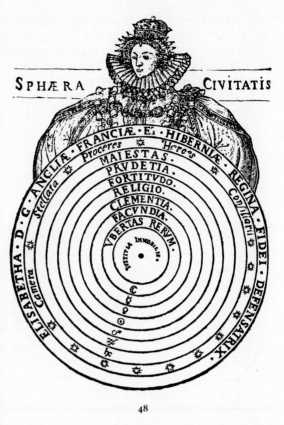

SPHÆRA CIVITATIS

48

47

If the body be so fearfully and wonderfully 49 made, what may we say, what may we not say, of the Soul for whom it was made—the quickener and mover of this engine, inhabitant of this house, life of this earth, light of this orb, and (may it be soberly construed) a little God in this little World? The soul and not the body is the man. God the efficient framed it, not of earth, of elements, of heavenly, of any matter, but, to show His infinite power, made his greatest works, this greatest work, of nothing, and vouch-safed himself to be the samplar and prototype—that, as the body is an express image and brief compendium of the world, so the soul is a vive representation and model of the glorious Trinity in incomprehensible unity, made—not the image, which is Christ's prerogative, and to be made had made it not the image of the eternal, but—*ad imaginem*, in or after that image whose perfections it doth, not without imperfection, resemble.

21

50   The soul of man hath three powers. One is called the life vegetable, in the which man is partner with trees and with plants. The second power is the life sensible, in the which a man is partner with beasts, for why all beasts have lives sensible. The third is called soul reasonable, by the which a man differeth from all other things, for there is none reasonable but man.

51   God alone excepted, who actually and everlastingly is whatsoever he may be, and which cannot hereafter be that which now he is not, all other things besides are somewhat in possibility, which as yet they are not in act. And for this cause there is in all things an appetite or desire whereby they incline to something which they may be, and, when they are it, they shall be perfecter than now they are. All which perfections are contained under the general name of Goodness. And because there is not in the world any thing whereby another may not some way be made the perfecter, therefore all things that are, are good.

Again, sith there can be no goodness desired which proceedeth not from God himself, as from the supreme cause of all things, and every effect doth after a sort contain, at leastwise resemble, the cause from which it proceedeth, all things in the world are said in some sort to seek the highest and to covet more or less the participation of God himself. Yet this doth nowhere so much appear as it doth in man.

The Queen's Subjects

FOREIGN visitors to England in the sixteenth century frequently noted three things—the pride and careless vitality of the people, their wealth and their rich apparel. The reign of Elizabeth had inherited from earlier times a tradition in attire which made the outward appearance of men correspond to their status in society, and to a certain extent this tradition endured into the seventeenth century. But a new individualism, combined with a vast increase in material treasure, was rapidly overwhelming the standard patterns of dress.

In most ages costume gives an external indication of the spirit of the time, and such indications were perhaps more emphatic among Elizabethans than among any others. The confusion between apparel by 'degree' and apparel by personal fancy was observed by many; and, besides this, comment was constant concerning the Englishman's passionate desire for variety. In effect, the basis of male costume consisted of doublet and hose, but from all corners of the earth such ornaments were imported as tended to engulf this simple foundation. France, Spain, Italy, even the East, made their contributions, and regularly these contributions were carried to extremes. Now, ruffs convoluted out like organ-pipes; now, falling bands became curious and rare; now, doublets swelled forwards like peascods. The Queen gave the lead to her ladies for ornate array in farthingales, and courtiers rejoiced in an almost feminine devotion to the niceties of dress. The contrast between a young gallant's jewels or ear-rings and his true valiancy is, in a sense, the measure of the age.

Those who looked back on the old days deplored the way in which country gentlemen, for the sake of silks and brocades, were ruining their estates and losing interest in antique hospitality; yet this display, this ostentatious richness, this variety, are the outward expression of that inner vitality which we recognize as the prime quality of Elizabethan times.

52

53 The nature of our nation is free, stout, hault, prodigal of life and blood.

54 Englishmen, especially being young and un-experienced, are apt to take all things in snuff.

55 Seldom shall you see any of my countrymen above eighteen or twenty years old to go without a dagger at the least at his back or by his side, although they be aged burgesses or magistrates of any city who in appearance are most exempt from brabling and contention. Our nobility wear commonly swords or rapiers with their daggers, as doth every common servingman also that followeth his lord and master.

56 The English are grave like the Germans, lovers of show; followed wherever they go by whole troops of servants, who wear their masters' arms in silver fastened to their left arms.

What be these tall fellows of whom you speak? 57
'They be our servingmen, that attend upon our table, and follow us in the streets when we be at London or any other great town, and furnish our halls at home.'
But, I pray you, have they no other qualities wherein to serve you, or do you use them for no other purpose than attend on your table, or follow you as shadows?
'Surely, no: neither is it the manner to offer them any labour or drudgery, for thereof they would take great scorn, being comely personages and commonly the sons of some honest yeomen or farmers of the country.'
Then can I compare them to monks and fat friars, who under pretence of prayer won themselves a lazy life and lived upon others' labour: so these men, being called men of service, do nothing less than serve.
'Do you say so, sir? Were it for the worship of a gentleman having good land and revenues to keep no more servants than, as they do in cities, those that for their necessary uses they must needs employ? If we gentlemen should so do, how should we furnish our halls? How should we be ready for quarrelers? Or how should our wives be waited on when they ride abroad, as commonly their custom is, chiefly in summer, the fair season and hunting-time? Besides them we have sub-servingmen, as I may call them, seldom in sight—as bakers, brewers, chamberlains, wardrobers, falconers, hunters, housekeepers, lackeys, and, for the most part, a natural fool or jester to make us sport; also a cook, with a scullion or two, launderers, hinds and hogherds, with some other silly slaves as I know not how to name them.'
I thought I had known all the retinue of a nobleman's or gentleman's house, but now I find I do not; for it seemeth a whole army or camp. And yet shall I tell you truly what I think: this last number, though it be least, is the more necessary sort of servants, because they serve necessity, and the other superfluity, or, I may call it, ambition.

MARGERE
DVTCHESS OF
NORFOLK 2 WIFE
THO D OF NORFOLK
HO WAS BEHEADED Y
OF QVEEN ELIZABETH
AVGHTER HEIR TO
O L AVDLEY

61   For by them oftentimes their masters are encouraged unto unlawful exactions of their tenants, their friends brought unto poverty by their rents enhanced, and they themselves brought to confusion by their own prodigality and errors, as men that, having not wherewith of their own to maintain their excesses, do search in highways, budgets, coffers, mails and stables which way to supply their wants. How divers of them also, coveting to bear an high sail, do insinuate themselves with young gentlemen and noblemen newly come to their lands, the case is too much apparent, whereby the good natures of the parties are not only a little impaired but also their livelihoods and revenues so wasted and consumed that, if at all yet not in many years, they shall be able to recover themselves. It were very good therefore that the superfluous heaps of them were in part diminished. And sith necessity enforceth to have some, yet let wisdom moderate their numbers, so shall their masters be rid of unnecessary charge and the commonwealth of many thieves. No nation cherisheth such store of them as we do here in England, in hope of which maintenance many give themselves to idleness that otherwise would be brought to labour and live in order like subjects.

62   The people are bold, courageous, ardent and cruel in war, fiery in attack and having little fear of death. They are not vindictive, but very inconstant, rash, vainglorious, light and deceiving, and very suspicious, especially of foreigners, whom they despise. They are full of courtly and affected manners and words, which they take for gentility, civility and wisdom. They are eloquent and very hospitable.

63   For this is strange—and yet how true it is none that ever travelled thither but can report—that it is always incident to an Englishman to think worst of his own nation either in learning, experience, common reason or wit, preferring always a stranger rather for the name than the wisdom.

64   Frankly to utter what I think of the incredible courtesy and friendliness in speech and affability used in this famous realm, I must needs confess it doth surmount and carry away the prick and prize of all others.

65   They excel in dancing and music, for they are active and lively, though of a thicker make than the French. They cut their hair close on the middle of the head, letting it grow on either side. They are good sailors and better pirates, cunning, treacherous and thievish. Above 300 are said to be hanged annually at London; beheading with them is less infamous than hanging. They give the wall as the place of honour. Hawking is the common sport with the gentry. They are more polite in eating than the French, consuming less bread but more meat, which they roast in perfection. They put a great deal of sugar in their drink. Their beds are covered with tapestry, even those of farmers.

They are powerful in the field, successful against their enemies; impatient of anything like slavery; vastly fond of great noises that fill the ear, such as the firing of cannon, drums and the ringing of bells—so that in London it is common for a number of them that have got a glass in their heads to go up into some belfry and ring the bells for hours together, for the sake of exercise. If they see a foreigner very well made or particularly handsome, they will say, 'It is a pity he is not an Englishman.'

66   We in England divide our people commonly into four sorts, as gentlemen, citizens or burgesses, yeomen, which are artificers, or labourers.

67   That infinite wisdom of God, which hath distinguished his angels by degrees, which hath given greater and less light and beauty to heavenly bodies, which hath made differences between beasts and birds, created the eagle and the fly, the cedar and the shrub, and, among stones, given the fairest tincture to the ruby and the quickest light to the diamond, hath also ordained kings, dukes or leaders of the people, magistrates, judges and other degrees among men.

68   It is lawful for the potestates, the nobility, the gentry, yeomanry, and for every private subject else, to wear attire every one in his degree, according as his calling and condition of life

requireth; yet a mean is to be kept, for *omne extremum vertitur in vitium*, every extreme is turned into vice. The nobility (though they have store of other attire) and the gentry (no doubt) may use a rich and precious kind of apparel (in the fear of God) to innoble, garnish and set forth their births, dignities, functions and callings; but for no other respect they may not in any manner of wise. As for the private subjects, it is not at any hand lawful that they should wear silks, velvets, satins, damasks, gold, silver and what they list. Now there is such a confuse mingle-mangle of apparel in England, and such preposterous excess thereof, as everyone is permitted to flaunt it out in what apparel he lust himself or can get by any kind of means. So that it is very hard to know who is noble, who is worshipful, who is a gentleman, who is not. This is a great confusion and a general disorder. God be merciful unto us!

69   In the general pride of England there is no fit difference made of degrees, for very bankrupts, players and cutpurses go apparelled like gentlemen.

70   The fantastical folly of our nation, even from the courtier to the carter, is such that no form of apparel liketh us longer than the first garment is in the wearing, if it continue so long and be not laid aside to receive some other trinket newly devised by the fickle-headed tailors, who covet to have several tricks in cutting, thereby to draw fond customers to more expense of money. Such is our mutability that today there is none to the Spanish guise, tomorrow the French toys are most fine and delectable, ere long no such apparel as that which is after the high Almaine fashion; by and by the Turkish manner is generally best liked of, otherwise the Morisco gowns, the Barbarian sleeves and the short French breeches make such a comely vesture that, except it were a dog in a doublet, you shall not see any so disguised as are my countrymen of England. And as these fashions are diverse, so likewise it is a world to see the costliness and the curiosity, the excess and the vanity, the pomp and the bravery, the change and the variety, and finally the fickle-

ness and the folly that is in all degrees, insomuch that nothing is more constant in England than inconstancy of attire.

How curious, how nice also, are a number of men and women, and how hardly can the tailor please them in making it fit for their bodies! How many times must it be sent back again to him that made it! What chafing, what fretting, what reproachful language doth the poor workman bear away! And many times when he doth nothing to it at all, yet when it is brought home again it is very fit and handsome; then must we put it on, then must the long seams of our hose be set by a plumb-line; then we puff, then we blow, and finally sweat till we drop, that our clothes may stand well upon us. I will say nothing of our heads, which sometimes are polled, sometimes curled, or suffered to grow at length like woman's locks, many times cut off above or under the ears, round as by a wooden dish. Neither will I meddle with our variety of beards, of which some are shaven from the chin like those of Turks, not a few cut short like to the beard of Marquess Otto, some made round like a rubbing brush, others with a *pique de vant* (O fine fashion!) or now and then suffered to grow long, the barbers being grown to be so cunning in this behalf as the tailors. And therefore if a man have a lean and straight face, a Marquess Otto's cut will make it broad and large; if it be platter-like, a long slender beard will make it seem the narrower; if he be weasel-becked, then much hair left on the cheeks will make the owner look big like a bowdled hen and so grim as a goose. Some lusty courtiers also and gentlemen of courage do wear either rings of gold, stones or pearl in their ears, whereby they imagine the workmanship of God not to be a little amended. But herein they rather disgrace than adorn their persons, as by their niceness in apparel, for which I say most nations do not unjustly deride us, as also for that we do seem to imitate all nations round about us, wherein we be like to the polypus or chameleon, and thereunto bestow most cost upon our arses, and much more than upon all the rest of our bodies, as women do likewise upon their heads and shoulders.

71 To begin first with their hats.

Sometimes they wear them sharp on the crown, perking up like a sphere or shaft of a steeple, standing a quarter of a yard above the crown of their heads, some more, some less, as please the fantasies of their minds. Othersome be flat and broad on the crown, like the battlements of a house. Another sort have round crowns, sometimes with one kind of band, sometime with another—now black, now white, now russet, now red, now green, now yellow, now this, now that, never content with one colour or fashion two days to an end. And thus in vanity they spend the Lord His treasure, consuming their golden years and silver days in wickedness and sin. And as the fashions be rare and strange, so are the things whereof their hats be made diverse also; for some are of silk, some of velvet, some of taffeta, some of sarcenet, some of wool, and, which is more curious, some of a certain kind of fine hair, far-fetched and dear-bought you may be sure; and so common a thing it is that every servingman, countryman and other, even all indifferently, do wear of these hats.

They have great and monstrous ruffs made either of cambric, holland, lawn or else of some other the finest cloth that can be got for money, whereof some be a quarter of a yard deep, yea, some more, very few less. Wot you what? The devil, as in the fulness of his malice, first invented these great ruffs, so hath he now found out also two great stays to bear up and maintain this his kingdom of great ruffs: the one is a certain kind of liquid matter which they call starch; the other pillar is a certain device made of wires, created for the purpose, whipped over either with gold thread, silver or silk, and this he calleth a supportass or underpropper.

Then have they hosen, which, as they be of divers fashions, so are they of sundry names. Some be called French-hose, some Gally-hose, and some Venetians. The French-hose are of two divers makings, for the common French-hose (as they list to call them) containeth length, breadth and sideness sufficient, and is made very round. The other containeth neither length, breadth nor sideness (being not past a quarter of a yard side), whereof some be paned, cut and drawn out with costly ornaments, with canions annexed reaching down beneath their knees.

The Gally-hosen are made very large and wide, reaching down to their knees only, with three or four guards a-piece laid down along either hose. And the Venetian-hosen, they reach beneath the knee to the gartering place of the leg. It is a small matter to bestow twenty nobles, ten pound, twenty pound, forty pound, yea, a hundred pound, of one pair of breeches.

Trust me, I hold this excessive costly apparel 72 a great cause why gentlemen cannot maintain their wonted and accustomed bounty and liberality in hospitality and housekeeping—for, whenas the mercer's book shall come, *item*, for so many yards of cloth of gold, of silver, velvet, satin, taffeta or suchlike ware; the goldsmith's *debet* for chains, rings, jewels, pearls and precious stones; the tailor's bill, so much for such a suit of laced satin and suchlike superfluous charges, amounting in one year to more than the revenues of his lands.

PORTRAITS IN PROSE AND VERSE

AN EARL

73 And then came my said Lord, the Earl of Leicester, by himself, apparelled all in white, his shoes of velvet, his stocks of hose knit silk, his upper stocks of white velvet lined with cloth of silver, his doublet of silver, his jerkin white velvet drawn with silver, beautified with gold and precious stone, his girdle and scabbard white velvet, his robe white satin embroidered with gold a foot broad very curiously, his cap black velvet with a white feather, his collar of gold beset with precious stones, and his garter about his leg of St George's order—a sight worthy the beholding.

6

A GALLANT

See you him yonder, who sits o'er the stage
With the tobacco-pipe now at his mouth?
It is Cornelius, that brave gallant youth,
Who is new printed to this fangled age.
He wears a jerkin cudgell'd with gold lace,
A profound slop, a hat scarce pipkin high,
For boots a pair of dag cases, his face
Furr'd with Cad's beard, his poinard on his
    thigh.
He wallows in his walk, his slop to grace,
Swears 'by the Lord', deigns no salutation
But to some jade that's sick of his own fashion—
As 'Farewell, sweet captain' or 'Boy, come
    apace'.
    Yet this Sir Bevis, or the Fairy Knight,
    Puts up the lie because he durst not fight.

7

AN APPLESQUIRE

After him followed two pert applesquires. The
one had a murrey-cloth gown on, faced down
before with gray cony and laid thick on the
sleeves with lace, which he quaintly bare up to
show his white taffeta hose and black silk
stockings. A huge ruff about his neck wrapped
in his great head like a wicker cage, a little hat
with brims like the wings of a doublet, wherein
he wore a jewel of glass, as broad as the chancery
seal. After him followed two boys in cloaks like
butterflies, carrying one of them his cutting
sword of choler, the other his dancing rapier of
delight. His camerard that bare him company
was a jolly light-timbered jackanapes in a suit of
watchet taffeta cut to the skin, with a cloak all
to-be-daubed with coloured lace.

A USURER

At length (as Fortune served) I lighted upon an
old straddling usurer, clad in a damask cassock
edged with fox fur, a pair of trunk slops sagging
down like a shoemaker's wallet, and a short
threadbare gown on his back, faced with moth-
eaten budge; upon his head he wore a filthy
coarse biggin, and next it a garnish of nightcaps
which a sage button-cap, of the form of a cow-
sherd, overspread very orderly. A fat chuff it
was, I remember, with a gray beard cut short to

the stumps as though it were grimed, and a huge
worm-eaten nose, like a cluster of grapes hanging
downward.

℃The fyrst chapter treateth of the naturall dysposition
of an Englyſhman, and of the noble realme of
England, ⁊ of the money that there is vſed.

℃I am an Engliſhman, and naked I ſtand here
Muſyng in my mynde, what rayment I ſhal were
For now I wyll were thys and now I wyl were that
Now I wyl were I cannot tel what
All new faſhyons, be pleſaunt to me
I wyl haue them, whether I thryue or thee
Now I a naked man, all men doth on me looke
What ſhould I do, but ſet cocke on the hoope
What do I care, yf all the worlde me fayle
I wyll get a garment, ſhal reche to my tayle
℃Than I am a minion, for I were the new gyſe
℃The

A MERCHANT'S WIFE

Mistress Minx, a merchant's wife, that will eat
no cherries, forsooth, but when they are at
twenty shillings a pound; that looks as simperingly
as if she were besmeared, and jets it as gingerly
as if she were dancing the Canaries. She is so
finical in her speech as though she spake nothing
but what she had first sewed over before in her
samplers, and the puling accent of her voice is
like a feigned treble or one's voice that interprets
to the puppets. What should I tell how squeamish
she is in her diet, what toil she puts her poor
servants unto to make her looking-glasses in the

pavement, how she will not go into the fields to cower on the green grass but she must have a coach for her convoy, and spends half a day in pranking herself if she be invited to any strange place?

A BROKER

There was coming alongst the valley towards us a square-set fellow, well fed and as briskly apparelled in a black taffeta doublet and a spruce leather jerkin with crystal buttons, a cloak faced afore with velvet and a Coventry cap of the finest wool; his face something ruby blush, cherry-cheeked like a shred of scarlet, or a little darker, like the lees of old claret wine. This fiery-faced churl had upon his fingers as many gold rings as would furnish a goldsmith's shop or beseem a pander of long profession to wear.

Wondering what companion this should be, I enquired of what occupation he was. 'Marry, sir,' quoth he, 'a broker.'

A WHEELWRIGHT

There dwelled in Grantchester, hard by Cambridge, a man called Tomkins, a wheelwright he was, and such a one as lived by his art; who, being a young man and unmarried, held it a

religion every Sunday to frolic it in the church-yard. His doublet was of leather, russeted after the best fashion, fair trussed afore with a dozen and a half of pewter buttons; a jerkin of gray kersey, with a tagged welt of the own, and, because his doublet was new, his sleeves hung down very properly; a round slop of white, with two guards about the pocket hole, graced with a long stock that, for wearing at the knee, were fenced with two pieces of a calf's skin. His ruff was of fine lockram, stitched very fair with Coventry blue; a green hat fresh from the haber-dashers, tied up before, and a brooch of copper, wherein St George sat very well mounted.

A FARMER'S DAUGHTER

A bonny lass she was, very well tucked up in a russet petticoat, with a bare hem and no fringe, yet had she a red lace and a stomacher of tuffed mockado, and a partlet cast over with a pretty whip; and dressed she was in a kerchief of holland, for her father was a farmer. Her kirtle was green, and at that hung a large leather purse with fair threaden tassels, and a new pair of yellow gloves, tufted with red raw silk very richly.

35

87

88

89

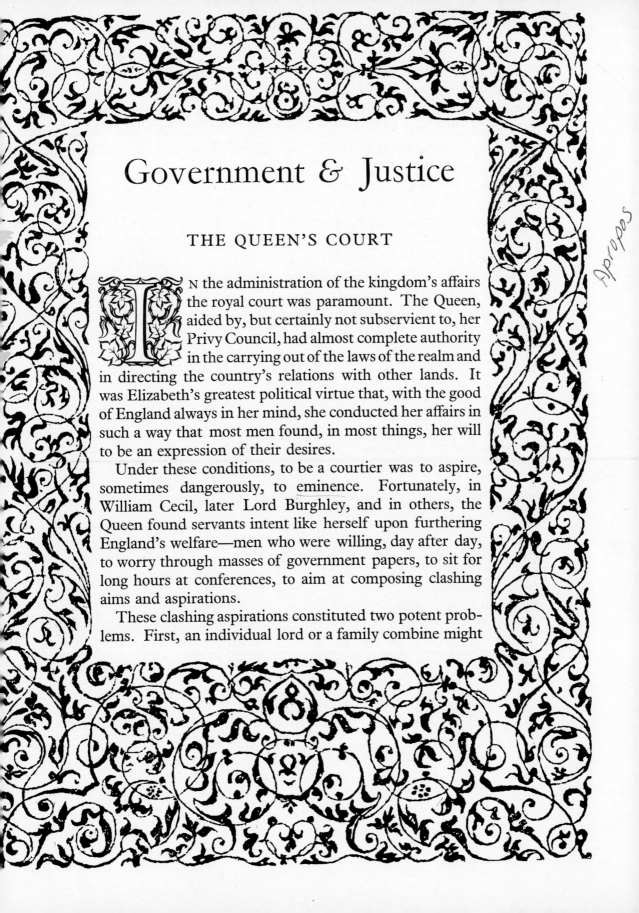

Government & Justice

THE QUEEN'S COURT

IN the administration of the kingdom's affairs the royal court was paramount. The Queen, aided by, but certainly not subservient to, her Privy Council, had almost complete authority in the carrying out of the laws of the realm and in directing the country's relations with other lands. It was Elizabeth's greatest political virtue that, with the good of England always in her mind, she conducted her affairs in such a way that most men found, in most things, her will to be an expression of their desires.

Under these conditions, to be a courtier was to aspire, sometimes dangerously, to eminence. Fortunately, in William Cecil, later Lord Burghley, and in others, the Queen found servants intent like herself upon furthering England's welfare—men who were willing, day after day, to worry through masses of government papers, to sit for long hours at conferences, to aim at composing clashing aims and aspirations.

These clashing aspirations constituted two potent problems. First, an individual lord or a family combine might attain such pre-eminence as to menace royalty itself. With characteristic acumen Elizabeth constantly endeavoured to balance one force against another, and when, for example, an Earl of Essex threatened to press his claims by force, she was prepared, even at personal sacrifice, to impose the final penalty. Her successor, James, had particular favourites at court; it might almost be said that Elizabeth maintained a whole court of favourites—and in their number lay strength. The second problem was one of patronage. Inevitably, those who sought to live at court looked round for lords sufficiently powerful to give them aid and protection and this meant that those less fortunate than others bitterly inveighed against the flatteries and fawnings of court life. 'Colin Clout's Come Home Again' is only one among many contemporary complaints. Such complaints, however, rarely reached the intensity of those written in James' reign, and never did the bitterness expressed in prose and verse direct itself towards the person of the Queen as the later bitterness penetrated beyond the orbit of particular lords towards the person of the King. With consummate art Elizabeth kept majesty enthroned in lonely splendour.

90

Each of these hath his part and administration in judgments, corrections of defaults, in election of offices, in appointing and collection of tributes and subsidies, or in making laws.

The Prince hath absolutely in his power the authority of war and peace, to defy what prince it shall please him and to bid him war, and again to reconcile himself and enter into league or truce with him at his pleasure or the advice only of his Privy Council. His Privy Council be chosen also at the Prince's pleasure out of the nobility or barony, and of the knights and esquires, such and so many as he shall think good, who doth consult daily, or when need is, of the weighty matters of the realm, to give therein to their Prince the best advice they can. The Prince doth participate to them all, or so many of them as he shall think good, such legations and messages as come from foreign princes, such letters or occurrents as be sent to himself or to his secretaries, and keepeth so many ambassades and letters sent unto him secret as he will.

The Prince useth also absolute power in crying

93 Generally to speak of the common wealth or policy of England, it is governed, administered and manured by three sorts of persons—the Prince, Monarch and head governor, which is called the King, or, if the crown fall to a woman, the Queen absolute, in whose name and by whose authority all things are administered; the Gentlemen, which be divided into two parts, the Barony or Estate of Lords, containing barons and all that be above the degree of a baron, and those which be no lords, as knights, esquires and simply gentlemen; the third and last sort of persons is named the yeomanry.

94

40

and decreeing the money of the realm by his proclamation only.

The Prince hath the wardship and first marriage of all those that hold lands of him in chief.

To be short, the Prince is the life, the head and the authority of all things that be done in the realm of England.

96 First, I must tell you of the grave and wise counsellors, whose foresight in peace warranteth safety in war, whose provision in plenty maketh sufficient in dearth, whose care in health is, as it were, a preparative against sickness. How great their wisdom hath been in all things the twenty-two years' peace doth both show and prove.

97 The court of England is in these days one of the most renowned and magnificent courts that are to be found in Europe.

98 What is a courtier?

'An attendant upon majesty, a companion of nobility, a friend to virtue and a hope of honour.'

My first day's walk was to the court, 100
    Where beauty fed mine eyes:
Yet found I that the courtly sport
    Did mask in sly disguise.
For falsehood sat in fairest looks
    And friend to friend was coy;
Court favour fill'd but empty books
    And there I found no joy.
Desert went naked in the cold,
    When crouching craft was fed;
Sweet words were cheaply bought and sold,
    But none that stood in stead.
Wit was employed for each man's own,
    Plain meaning came too short.
All these devises seen and known
    Made me forsake the court.

The seas, you say, are uncertain: but he that 101 sails in your court seas shall find 'hem ten times fuller of hazard; wherein to see what is to be seen is torment more than a free spirit can endure; but, when you come to suffer, how many injuries swallow you! What care and devotion must you use to humour an imperious lord, proportion your looks to his looks, smiles to his smiles—fit your sails to the wind of his breath!

103

104

105

43

Government & Justice

THE HIGH COURT OF PARLIAMENT & THE COURTS OF LAW

ALTHOUGH all administrative power resided in the prince, Parliament, or rather the High Court of Parliament, was no mere cypher. Here the laws were fashioned; here was the prime seat of justice. Elizabeth might boldly defy Parliamentary wishes, as she did for years over the vexed question of marriage and succession; she might even scold the members when they acted against her expressed wishes; yet Parliament was jealous of its privileges and played a powerfully important part in framing the model of Elizabethan life.

Connected with it were the other courts, simply housed in corners of the great hall at Westminster, wherein justices endeavoured, with the best will that in them lay, to administer the law equably. They did not entirely succeed, it is true, for bribery and the power of lordly influence were rife, but, when we relate England to other lands in this time, we must admit that on the whole the aims and the practices of the English law maintained a high standard. Penalties were severe, but they were governed by contemporaries' judgment of the crimes; torture was not permitted save in cases of treason; if there were many hangings and if the prisons were full, we must remember that the men of this time were hot-blooded and impatiently inclined to take the law into their own hands. No doubt lawyers made a fat living out of their work in the courts, but there would have been no such fat living had their fellow-citizens not been angrily litigious by nature and violent in their actions.

107 The most high and absolute power of the realm of England consisteth in the Parliament. For every Englishman is intended to be there present, either in person or by procuration and attornies, of what pre-eminence, state, dignity or quality soever he be, from the Prince (be he King or Queen) to the lowest person of England.

In the great hall at Westminster he (Henry III) 108 ordained three judgment seats, to wit, at the entry on the right hand the common place, where civil matters are to be pleaded, specially such as touch lands or contracts; at the upper end of the hall, on the right hand, or south-east corner, the King's Bench, where pleas of the Crown have

45

from 9 of the clock till it be 11, do sit. This place is called the Star Chamber because the roof thereof is decked with the likeness of stars gilt: there be plaints heard of riots, routs and other misdemeanours. Then at the upper end of the great hall by the King's Bench is a going up to a great chamber, called the White Hall, wherein is now kept the Court of Wards and Liveries; and adjoining thereunto is the Court of Requests.

There are also sundry usual courts holden once in every quarter of the year, which we commonly call terms, of the Latin word *terminus*, wherein all controversies are determined that happen within the Queen's dominions. These are commonly holden at London, except upon some great occasion they be transferred to other places. How well they are followed by suitors the great wealth of lawyers without any travail of mine can readily express. For, as after the coming of the Normans the nobility had the start, and after them the clergy, so now all the wealth of the land doth flow unto our common lawyers, of whom some one, having practised little above thirteen or fourteen years, is able to buy a purchase of so many one thousand pounds—which argueth that they wax rich apace, and will be richer if their clients become not the more wiser and wary hereafter.

their hearing, and on the left hand, or south-west corner, sitteth the Lord Chancellor, accompanied with the Master of the Rolls and with certain other of the eleven men learned for the most part in the civil law, and called Masters of the Chancery.

Within the port or entry into the hall on either side are ascendings up into large chambers without the hall adjoining thereunto, wherein certain Courts be kept: namely, on the right hand is the Court of the Exchequer, a place of account for the revenues of the Crown. In this Court be heard those that are delators, or informers, in popular and penal actions. On the left hand above the stair is the Dutchy chamber, wherein is kept the Court for the Dutchy of Lancaster. Then is there in another chamber the office of receipts of the Queen's revenues for the Crown. Then is there also the Star Chamber where, in the term time every week once at the least, which is commonly on Fridays and Wednesdays, and on the next day after the term endeth, the Lord Chancellor and the Lords and other of the Privy Council, and the two Chief Justices of England,

One asked a fellow what Westminster Hall was like. 'Marry,' quoth the other, 'it is like a butler's box at Christmas amongst gamesters, for, whosoever loseth, the box will be sure to be a winner.'

My skill is unable to render due reverence to the honourable judges according to their worthiness but especially at this instant as the benches are now supplied, neither would I eclipse the honest reputation of a number of learned lawyers that are to be held in a reverend regard and that are to be honoured and esteemed; yet amongst these there be a number of others that do multiply suits and draw on quarrels between friend and friend, between brother and brother, and sometimes between the father and the son.

There be too many lawyers, especially of those attorneys, solicitors and such other pettifoggers,

whereof there be such abundance that the one of them can very hardly thrive by the other. And this multitude of them do trouble all the parts of England.

115 There are in London, and within the buildings that round about touch her sides and stand within her reach, thirteen strong houses of sorrow, where the prisoner hath his heart wasting away sometimes a whole prenticeship of years in cares. They are most of them built of freestone, but none are free within them; cold are their embracements, unwholesome is their cheer; despairful their lodgings, uncomfortable their societies, miserable their inhabitants. O what a deal of wretchedness can make shift to lie in a little room!

I no sooner was entered into this Infernal 116 Island (where many men lie wind-bound sometimes four or five years together), but a fellow (whom at first sight I took to be a gardener, because he had somewhat a reddish beard and turned up withal) called me to a book (no Bible or Divinity, but rather of Negromancy, for all the prisoners called it the Black Book). Coming to it, he demanded my name: I told him, and then he set it down as horses are in Smithfield at the Tolbooth. This ceremony being ended, he asked me whether I would go to the Masterside, the Knights' Ward, or any other place of a cheaper rate. I answered the best, though it were the dearest, for I did hope to get my liberty before a week was expired. Upon this determination there was one called to show me the way to my lodging, who upon the first call made no delay, but instantly came waddling downstairs. He was

(with a countenance as sour as any mustard-maker in the city) bade me welcome, and told me that there was a garnish to be paid—but I that understood the Hebrew, the Syriac or Chaldean language as well as his speech, asked him what that was: he told me two shillings would discharge it. I mildly certified him I was not at that unhappy present so well furnished, besides, I was ignorant whether any such thing were due to him or no. At this answer, he roused himself up like an angry mastiff and, being in choler, in a currish manner barked out these words to me: 'Sir, if you mean to lie on this side, you must and shall pay me my fees, or (though you be no alderman) I will be so bold as to uncloak you.'

In London, and other such places, it would 118 move a stony heart to hear one crying up and down the streets, 'Bread and meat for the poor prisoners of Newgate, for Christ Jesus' sake!', and the prisoners crying out of their grates and holes, 'One penny or half-penny, for Christ his sake, to buy some bread, to buy some bread!'

a gross fellow, one that had a fat body though a lean brain, a face of a sanguine complexion and an heart correspondent to the same; he had a motley beard cut round like a rubbing brush, so that if all the skin of his body had been like that of his face, it would have served excellent well when he had been dead to make cloakbags of. This lump of man's flesh (that like a foreman of a jury could speak nothing so well as guilt) conveyed me up a pair of stairs, and so to a door, where another Fury like himself sat, telling me that, if I meant to have entrance there, I must pay my fees or else I could have no farther passage that way. A shilling was his demand, which he would have or else I must return the same way I came. I, seeing nothing but a silver key would open this lock, gave him his fee. My corpulent conductor brought me through a little gallery, which led us to a spacious room and then into a hall hung round about with the story of the Prodigal Child (a very edifying piece of workmanship for the guests of that place). Being come into this uncouth and strange place, my guide

Some broken Breade and meate for y.ᵉ poore prisnors for the Lords sake pitter the poore 119

If a woman poison her husband, she is burned 120 alive; if the servant kill his master, he is to be executed for petty treason; he that poisoneth a man is to be boiled to death in water or lead, although the party die not of the practice; in cases of murder all the accessories are to suffer pains of death accordingly. Perjury is punished by the pillory, burning in the forehead with the letter P, the rewalting of the trees growing upon the grounds of the offenders, and loss of all his movables. Many trespasses also are punished by the cutting off one or both ears from the head of the offender, as the utterance of seditious words against the magistrates, fray-makers, petty robbers, etc. Rogues are burned through the ears; carriers of sheep out of the land, by the loss of their hands.

The greatest and most grievous punishment 12 used in England for such as offend against the state is drawing from the prison to the place of execution upon an hurdle or sled, where they are hanged till they be half dead, and then taken down and quartered alive; after that, their members and bowels are cut from their bodies and thrown into a fire provided near hand and within their own sight, even for the same purpose.

122

123 In no place shall you see malefactors go more constantly, more assuredly and with less lamentation to their death than in England.

The Church

O N 28 April 1559, Parliament passed a Bill of Uniformity, and this was followed, the next day, by a Bill of Supremacy in which Elizabeth was made 'Supreme Governer' of the realm in spiritual affairs. Immediately all the bishops save one vacated their sees, accompanied by a number of the minor clergy.

But no martyrs were made. Catholics had been executed in the past, and Mary Tudor had steeped her hands deep in Protestant blood. Elizabeth was determined on another policy. As Parliament after Parliament sought, by means direct and indirect, to ensure the application of extreme penalties upon those of the old faith, her power of veto was repeatedly applied and at times her stinging words lashed out at those who attempted to force their will upon the country. She knew well enough that puritans, whether arrayed in Rome's splendid panoply or clad in Geneva's drab gowns, were the very devil: such men wanted only that all should be forced to bow to their particular creeds. So it was that when Sir Francis Walsingham begged her to prosecute Catholics more sternly, 'I make no windows into the souls of men', she said.

Thus, for the first years of her reign she was confronted by little serious religious opposition translated into political terms; and, in addition, by her adroit diplomacy she succeeded largely in keeping her European neighbours at guess or, at least, in hope.

The outbreak of war with Spain brought changed conditions. Jesuit priests made it part of their faith to seek her destruction, and at the same time the more fanatic sects of Puritanism began to flourish apace. Even to the end of her reign, however, the queen kept to her chosen path and in Richard Hooker's great *Lawes of ecclesiasticall politie*, issued between 1594 and 1597, she welcomed a profound philosophical defence of the church she had nurtured and reared.

Worthy prelates aided her, but their devoted efforts were not sufficient to eradicate the many evils which might be found among the minor clergy. Many vicars were ignorant and lazy; and the curse of simony was widespread. Despite this, the record of the church during the age was one not without honour; its characteristic form maintained, in social, political and spiritual thought, a balance which, lost, could well have been calculated to send the country crashing to destruction. After looking at the martyr-anxious eyes of Catholic fanatics and the hard, bitter gaze of the Puritan bigots, it is good to turn to the more measured mien of some among Elizabeth's distinguished bishops. There is a virtue in liberalism when the dark forces of zealotry are rife.

124

125 There are in this isle two and twenty bishops, which are as it were superintendents over the Church, men of great zeal and deep knowledge, diligent preachers of the word, earnest followers of their doctrine, careful watchmen that the wolf devour not the sheep, in civil government politic, in ruling the spiritual sword (as far as to them under their Prince appertaineth) just, cutting off those members from the Church by rigour that are obstinate in their heresies and instructing those that are ignorant, appointing godly and learned ministers in every of their sees, that in their absence may be lights to such as are in darkness, salt to those that are unsavoury, leaven to such as are not seasoned.

Visitations are holden oftentimes, whereby abuses and disorders, either in the laity for negligence or in the clergy for superstition or in all for wicked living, there are punishments, by due execution whereof the divine service of God is honoured with more purity and followed with greater sincerity.

126 There are also another sort of simoniacal lepers, such as be patrons of benefices, who, having power to appoint a godly, learned and discreet pastor to the congregation and church, whereof they ought indeed to be patrons, that is to say, careful and provident fathers, yet never-

theless, seeking after their own private gain rather than the gaining of men's souls, do, contrary to the law of God and man, sell their benefices and donations for money. And so, refusing to admit those which be worthy but preferring those which be unworthy, they call to the inheritance of God's sanctuary schismatics, seditious persons, atheists, ignorant and unlearned asses, flatterers and sometime their own kinsmen and familiars, how unmeet soever.

9   Fain would I have a living, if I could tell how to come by it.

Echo: Buy it.

Buy it, fond echo? Why, thou dost greatly mistake it.

Echo: Stake it.

Stake it? What should I stake at this game of simony?

Echo: Money.

What, is the world a game? Are livings gotten by playing?

Echo: Paying.

Paying? But say, what's the nearest way to come by a living?

Echo: Giving.

Must his worship's fists be needs then oiled with angels?

Echo: Angels.

Take an odd vicar in a village town,   131
   That only prays for plenty and for peace,
If he can get him but a threadbare gown,
   And tythe a pig, and eat a goose in grease,
   And set his hand unto his neighbour's lease,
And bid the clerk on Sundays ring the bell,
He is a churchman fits the parish well.

And for my parishioners, they are a kind of 132 people that love a pot of ale better than a pulpit, and a corn-rick better than a church-door, who, coming to divine service more for fashion than devotion, are contented after a little capping and kneeling, coughing and spitting, to help me to sing out a psalm, and sleep at the second lesson, or awake to stand up at the gospel, and say 'Amen' at the peace of God, and stay till the banns of matrimony be asked, or till the clerk have cried a pied stray bullock, a black sheep or a gray mare, and then, for that some dwell far off, be glad to be gotten home to dinner.

London

THE CITY

THE shores of the Strand and a half-ring marked by a line of posterns running from the Tower, symbol of royal command, through Aldgate, Bishopsgate, Moorgate, Cripplegate and Aldergate on to Temple Bar—within this semicircle the city was enclosed. New houses were rapidly obscuring the original walls of fortification, nearby villages were becoming engulfed, and across the river Southwark, with its theatres, was easy of access; but there were open fields between London and Westminster, green hills to the north and countryside to the east.

Here was the living symbol of the age's paradox. Palaces, towers and theatres, fair houses with ample gardens, evil-smelling slums and a babel of rude noises; the song of the thrush and the harsh grating of cart-wheels; high thoughts, rich poetic fancies and rascally cozenings; sharp class distinctions and a peculiar sense of unity; rich splendour and miserable degradation. 'Thou hast all things in thee to make thee fairest,' wrote a poet, 'And all things in thee to make thee foulest; for thou art attir'd like a bride, drawing all that look upon thee to be in love with thee, but there is much harlot in thine eyes.' Here usurers racked the gay young gallants; here Greene died on a pauper's bed, repenting his sins; here worthy preachers sought at Paul's Cross to attract the attention of the motley crew who strutted, for fashion's sake or for the sake of their own criminal purposes, up and down the cathedral's middle aisle; here bulls and bears were miserably baited and Shakespeare made glorious the stage. If the city's streets were dirty, the Strand was softly lapped by the waters of the Thames, still a fair and crystal stream—'the broad river of Thames', an Italian visitor styled it, 'most charming and quite full of swans white as snow'—at once a messenger from rural England, a highway served by scores of boatmen and a point of departure whence adventurous souls set out for mysterious Cathay and the Virginia paradise. And for those who stayed at home the wonder of London Bridge outvied the wonder of Arno's bridges and the Rialto in Venice.

54

133

wool, most durable against the force of the water, and not to be repaired but upon great fall of the waters and by artificial turning or stopping the recourse of them. Or if men respect the houses built upon the bridge, as great and high as those of the firm land, so as a man cannot know that he passeth a bridge, but would judge himself to be in the street, save that the houses on both sides are combined in the top, making the passage somewhat dark, and that in some few open places the river of Thames may be seen on both sides.

137 Omitting to speak of great ships and other vessels of burden, there pertaineth to the cities of London, Westminster and borough of Southwark above the number, as is supposed, of 2000 wherries and other small boats, whereby 3000 poor men at the least be set on work and maintained.

134 Thou noblest city of the now noblest nation.

135 London, a place both for the beauty of building, infinite riches, variety of all things, that excelleth all the cities in the world, insomuch that it may be called the storehouse and mart of all Europe. Close by this city runneth the famous river called the Thames, which from the head where it riseth, named Isis, unto the fall midway it is thought to be an hundred and fourscore miles. What can there be in any place under the heavens that is not in this noble city either to be bought or borrowed?

It hath divers hospitals for the relieving of the poor, six-score fair churches for divine service, a glorious bourse which they call the Royal Exchange, for the meeting of merchants of all countries where any traffic is to be had. And among all the strange and beautiful shows me thinketh there is none so notable as the bridge which crosseth the Thames.

136 The Bridge at London is worthily to be numbered among the miracles of the world, if men respect the building and foundation, laid artificially and stately over an ebbing and flowing water upon twenty-one piles of stone, with twenty arches under which barks may pass, the lowest foundation being (as they say) packs of

138 The Exchange, or public place for the meeting of merchants and for the selling of smaller or richer wares at London, being built of freestone by Sir Thomas Gresham, knight and merchant, is the most stately building in that kind that I have seen in Europe or Turkey.

139 At London the houses of the citizens (especially in the chief streets) are very narrow in the front towards the street but are built five or six roofs high, commonly of timber and clay with plaster, and are very neat and commodious within. And the building of citizens' houses in other cities is not much unlike this. But withall understand that in London many stately palaces, built by noblemen upon the river Thames, do make a very great show to them that pass by water, and that there be many more like palaces, also, built towards land, but scattered and great part of them in back lanes and streets, which, if they were joined to the first in good order, as other cities are built uniformly, they would make not only fair streets, but even a beautiful city, to which few might justly be preferred for the magnificence of the building. Besides, that the aldermen's and chief citizens' houses, howsoever they are stately for building, yet being built all inward that the whole room towards the streets may be reserved for shops of tradesmen, make no

55

show outwardly, so as in truth all the magnificence of London building is hidden from the view of strangers at the first sight, till they have more particular view thereof by long abode there; and then they will prefer the buildings of this famous city to many that appear more stately at the first sight.

141 The manner of the most gentlemen and noblemen also is to house themselves (if possible they may) in the suburbs of the city, because most commonly the air there being somewhat at large, the place is healthy, and through the distance from the body of the town the noise not much, and so consequently quiet.

142 Will you now go visit the shopkeepers that are so busy with their 'What lack you, sir?' or 'What is it you would have bought?' and let us take a good survey what the commodities be that they would thus set forth to sale, and we shall find

that, as Diogenes, passing through a fair, cried out 'O how many things are here to be vented that Nature hath no need of', so we may likewise say 'O how many gaudy trifles are here to be sold that are good for nothing but to maintain pride and vanity'.

The goldsmiths' shops at London in England 143 (being in divers streets but especially that called Cheapside) are exceedingly richly furnished continually with gold and silver plate, and jewels. The goldsmiths' shops upon the bridges at Florence and Paris have perhaps sometimes been as richly or better furnished, for the time of some nuptial feast of the princes or like occasion, with plate and jewels borrowed of private persons for that purpose; but I may lawfully say, setting all love of my country apart, that I did never see any such daily show, anything so sumptuous in any place of the world, as in London.

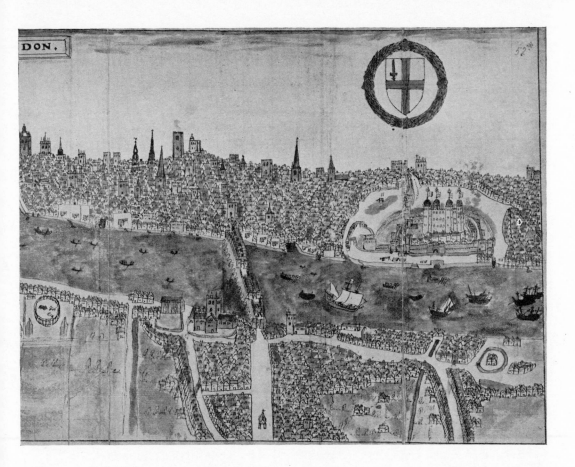

44   Men of trades and sellers of wares in this city have oftentimes changed their places, as they have found their best advantage. For whereas Mercers and Haberdashers used to keep their shops in West Cheap, of later time they held them on London Bridge, where partly they yet remain. The Goldsmiths of Gutherons-lane and Old Exchange are now for the most part removed into the south side of West Cheap; the Pepperers and Grocers of Sopers-lane are now in Bucklers-bury and other places. The Drapers of Lombard-street and of Cornhill are seated in Candlewick-street and Watling-street; the Skinners from St Mary Pellipers or at the Axe into Budge-row and Walbrook; the Stockfishmongers in Thames-street; Wet-fishmongers in Knightriders-street and Bridge-street; the Ironmongers of Iron-mongers-lane and Old Jury into Thames-street; the Vintners from the Vinetree into divers places.

But the Brewers for the most part remain near to the friendly water of Thames; the Butchers in Eastcheap and St Nicholas Shambles. The Hosiers of old time in Hosier-lane, near unto Smithfield, are since removed into Cordwainer-street, the upper part thereof by Bow Church, and last of all into Birchovers-lane by Cornhill. The Shoemakers and Curriers of Cordwainer-street removed the one to St Martins-le-Grand, the other to London Wall near unto Moorgate. Cooks or Pastelars for the more part in Thames-street, the other dispersed into divers parts. Poulters of late removed out of the Poultry be-twixt the Stocks and Great Conduit in Cheap into Grass-street and St Nicholas Shambles; Bowyers from Bowyers-row by Ludgate into divers places, and almost worn out with the Fletchers. Patten-makers of St Margaret, Pattens-lane, clean worn out.

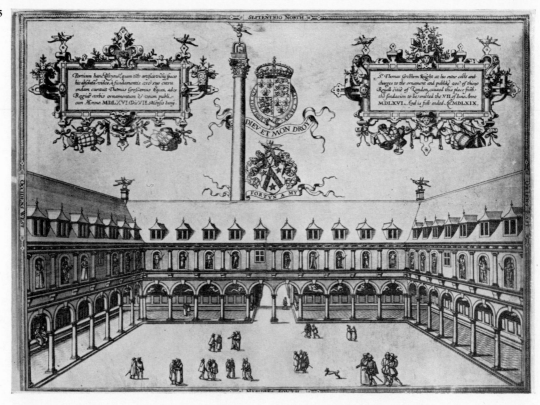

146 The number of cars, drays, carts and coaches more than hath been accustomed, the streets and lanes being straitened, must needs be dangerous, as daily experience proveth. The coachman rides behind the horse tails, lasheth them and looketh not behind him; the drayman sitteth and sleepeth on his dray and letteth his horse lead him home. I know that by the good laws and customs of this city shod carts are forbidden to enter the same except upon reasonable causes, as service of the prince or suchlike, they be tolerated; also that the fore-horse of every carriage should be led by hand—but these good orders are not observed. Now of late years the use of coaches brought out of Germany is taken up and made so common as there is neither distinction of time nor difference of persons observed; for the world runs on wheels with many whose parents were glad to go on foot.

147 Let me alone, I prithee, in this cell;
Entice me not into the city's hell.
What more variety of pleasures can
An idle city-walk afford a man?
More troublesome and tedious well I know
'Twill be into the peopled streets to go.
Witness that hotch-potch of so many noises,
Black-saunts of so many several voices, that
 chaos of rude sounds—that harmony
And diapason of harsh Barbary,
Compos'd of several mouths and several cries,
Which to men's ears turn both their tongues and
 eyes.
There squeaks a cart-wheel; here a tumbril
 rumbles;
Here scolds an old bawd; there a porter grumbles.
Here two tough car-men combat for the way;
There two for looks begin a coward fray.
Two swaggering knaves here brabble for a whore;
There brawls an ale-knight for his fat-grown
 score.

The city is the map of vanities,
The mart of fools, the magazine of gulls,
The painter's shop of antics.

148

149   Paul's Walk is the land's epitome.

150   For at one time, in one and the same rank—
yea, foot by foot and elbow by elbow—shall you
see walking the Knight, the Gull, the Gallant,
the Upstart, the Gentleman, the Clown, the
Captain, the Applesquire, the Lawyer, the
Usurer, the Citizen, the Bankrupt, the Scholar,
the Beggar, the Doctor, the Idiot, the Ruffian,
the Cheater, the Puritan, the Cut-throat, the
High-men, the Low-men, the True-man and
the Thief—of all trades and professions some,
of all countries some.

151   Walk in Paul's
And but observe the sundry kinds of shapes,
Thou'lt swear that London is as rich in apes
As Afric Tabraca. One wrys his face:
This fellow's wry neck is his better grace:
He, coined in newer mint of fashion,
With the right Spanish shrug shows passion.
There comes one in a muffler of Cadiz-beard,
Frowning as he would make the world afeard;

With him a troop all in gold-dawbèd suits,
Looking like Talbots, Percys, Montacutes—
As if their very countenances would swear
The Spaniard should conclude a peace for fear;
But bring them to a charge, then see the luck—
Though but a false fire, they their plumes will
    duck.
What marvel, since life's sweet?
O what a pageant's this! What fool was I
To leave my study to see vanity!
The further that we walk, more vanity
Presents itself to prospect of mine eye.
Here swears some seller, though a known un-
    truth;
Here his wife's baited by some quick-chapt
    youth.
There in that window Mistress Minx doth stand
And to some copesmate beckoneth her hand;
In is he gone, Saint Venus be his speed,
For some great thing must be adventurèd.
There comes a troop of puisnes from the play,
Laughing like wanton schoolboys all the way.
Yon go a knot to Bloom his ordinary.

152

First, having diligently enquired out an ordin- 153
ary of the largest reckoning, whither most of your
courtly gallants do resort, let it be your use to
repair thither some half hour after eleven; for
then you shall find most of your fashion-mongers
planted in the room waiting for meat.

Being arrived in the room, salute not any but
those of your acquaintance; walk up and down

Buy a steele or a Tinder Box

I haue fresh Cheese and Creame
I haue fresh

by the rest as scornfully and as carelessly as a gentleman-usher. Select some friend (having first thrown off your cloak) to walk up and down the room with you—let him be suited, if you can, worse by far than yourself, he will be a foil to you; and this will be a means to publish your clothes better than Paul's, a tennis-court or a playhouse. Discourse as loud as you can, no matter to what purpose if you but make a noise and laugh in fashion, and have a good sour face to promise quarrelling, you shall be much observed.

155   There is not so base a groom that comes into an alehouse to call for his pot but he must have his pipe of tobacco, for it is a commodity that is now as vendible in every tavern, inn and alehouse as either wine, ale or beer, and for apothecaries' shops, grocers' shops, chandlers' shops, they are (almost) never without company that from morning till night are still taking of tobacco.

There be 7000 shops in and about London that doth vent tobacco, as it is credibly reported that there be over and above that number.

156   They say this town is full of cozenage.

158   These shifters will come unto an inn or victualling house that is most used in the town, and walk up and down; and if there come any gentleman or other to lay up either cloak, sword or any other thing worth the having, then one of this crew taketh the marks of the thing or at least the token the party giveth them. Anon, after he is gone, he likewise goeth forth, and with a great countenance cometh in again to the maid or servant, calling for what another left. If they doubt to deliver it, then he frets and calls them at his pleasure and tells them the marks and tokens. Having thus done, he blames their forgetfulness and gives them a couple of pence to buy them pins, bidding them fetch it straight and know him better the next time; wherewith they are pleased and he possessed of his prey.

₁₆₀

so severe, such ugly, base and bold impieties dare show their faces? What an army of insufferable abuses, detestable vices, most damnable villainies, abominable pollutions, inexplicable mischiefs, sordid inquinations, horrible and hellhound-like-perpetrated flagitious enormities have been here mustered together!

₁₆₁ We few that were there did spend the same day about the searching out of sundry that were receptors of felons, where we found a great many as well in London, Westminster, Southwark, as in all other places about the same. Amongst our travels this one matter tumbled out by the way, that one Wotton, a gentleman-born and sometime a merchantman of good credit, who, falling by time into decay, kept an ale-house at Smart's Quay near Billingsgate, and after, for some misdemeanour being put down, he reared up a new trade of life, and in the same house he procured all the cut-purses about this city to repair to his said house. There was a school-house set up to learn young boys to cut purses. There were hung up two devices; the one was a pocket, the other was a purse. The pocket had in it certain counters and was hung about with hawks' bells and over the top did hang a little sacring bell; and he that could take out a counter without any noise was allowed to be a 'Public Foister'; and he that could take a piece of silver out of the purse without the noise of any of the bells, he was adjudged a 'Judicial Nipper'.

₁₆₂ Who would imagine that in a kingdom so fertile in all sorts of wholesome discipline there should grow up such rank and such pestilent beds of hemlock—that in the very heart of a state so rarely governed and dieted by good laws there should breed such loathsome and such ulcerous impostumes—that in a city so politic, so civil and

Unto the city next I went, ₁₆₃
Where liberally I launch'd and spent,
   As set on Fortune's lap.
The little stock I had in store
   Methought would ne'er be done;
Friends flock'd about me more and more,
   As quickly lost as won.
For when I spent, they then were kind,
   But when my purse did fail,
The foremost man came last behind—
   Thus love with wealth doth quail.
Once more for footing yet I strove,
   Although the world did frown;
But they before that held me up
   Together trod me down;
And lest once more I should arise,
   They sought my quite decay.
Then got I into this disguise
   And thence I stole away—
And in my mind, methought I said:
   'Lord! bless me from the city,
Where simpleness is thus betray'd,
   And no remorse or pity.'

₁₆₄

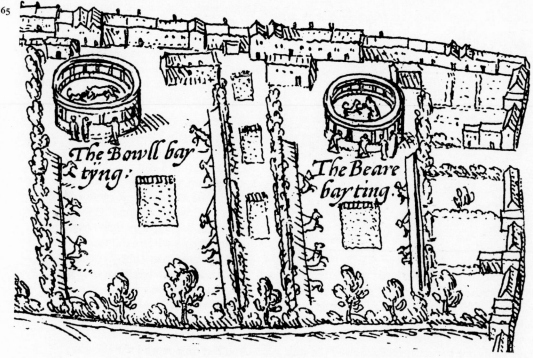

The Bowll bay-tyng.

The Beare bayting

THEATRES AND BEAR GARDENS

LONDON'S first permanent theatre was erected in 1576, but already the out-skirts of the city had their bear-baiting pits and outwardly the playhouses did not differ overmuch from these noisome yards. Puritans and hostile civic authorities treated both in the same way; the actors at times shared the same arena with the dogs and the bears; the great tragedian Alleyn was not ashamed to associate himself with the brutal sport. Although contemporary literature offers not a word in their defence, crowds flocked to the bear gardens and even the Queen took strange delight in these bloody spectacles.

Dirt, tumult and savagery—and side by side with them the theatre which became the poet's royal exchange, the glory by which the age is now best remembered. The crowd attending the Globe cannot have been much dissimilar to the crowd which clamoured in the hell of the Hope; yet silence miraculously descended as the prologue announced the play's first act and poetic melody bound the hearers by golden chains.

Avidly attracted by show, unafraid to display their passions, intensely interested in men, the Elizabethans found their truest artistic expression in the drama. Dark-minded Puritan fathers might fulminate against the moral iniquity of the stage and point to specific instances of God's wrath at transgressors; the mayor and aldermen might, with some show of reason, demonstrate the dangers of play-going in plague-time; but the trumpets still sounded from the roofs of the theatres, the comedies and the tragedies and the histories proceeded unchecked, and we are the richer by it.

166

167 Thou, O thou beautiful but bewitching city, by the wantonness of thine eye and the music of thy voice allurest people from all the corners of the land to throng in heaps at thy fairs and thy theatres.

168 We walked across the bridge to Southwark. Here there is a round building with three corridors built one above the other. Here there were close upon one hundred great English dogs, each of which had a special kennel made of boards. Here in a building three bears, each larger than the other, were baited one after another by some dogs. Then a horse was brought in, and it, too, was baited. Then an ox was led in. This ox offered a game resistance. Then out of a mechanical contrivance there came forth various males and females who danced, sang and spoke. Lastly a

man came out and scattered bread among the crowd, who scrambled for it. Finally, a rocket was shot into a rosette which hung above the place. From this rosette a heap of apples and pears fell upon the people who stood below gazing up at it. Then when the crowd was scrambling for the fruit there fell from the rosette a number of little rockets, whereat the people who were picking up the fruit were greatly scared, which was a mirth-provoking sight. Afterwards from all corners rockets and fireworks flew, wherewith the show came to an end.

Publius, student at the common law,   169
    Oft leaves his books, and for his recreation
To Paris Garden doth himself withdraw,
    Where he is ravish'd with such delectation
As down amongst the dogs and bears he goes;
    Where, whiles he skipping cries 'To head! To head!'
His satin doublet and his velvet hose
    Are all with spittle from above bespread—
Then he is like his father's country hall,
    Stinking with dogs and muted all with hawks.
And rightly too on him this filth doth fall,
    Which for such filthy sports his books forsakes,
Leaving old Plowden, Dyer and Brooke alone
To see old Harry Hunks and Sacarson.

The very noise of the place put me in mind of 170 hell.

Look but upon the common plays in London 171 and see the multitude that flocketh to them and followeth them! Behold the sumptuous theatre-houses, a continual monument of London's prodigality and folly!

172 Will not a filthy play, with the blast of a trumpet, sooner call thither a thousand than an hour's tolling of a bell bring to the sermon a hundred?

173 For my part I commend not such sour censurers, but I think in stage-plays may be much good, in well-penned comedies and specially tragedies. And I remember in Cambridge, howsoever the preciser sort have banished them, the wiser did and still do maintain them.

174 Our late Queen Elizabeth of blessed memory, rightly styled the world's Phoebe, among women a Sybilla, among queens a Sheba—how well she approved of these recreations, being as she termed them 'harmless spenders of time', the large exhibitions which she conferred on such as were esteemed notable in that kind may sufficiently witness. Neither did she hold it any derogation to that royal and princely majesty, which she then in her regal person presented, to give some countenance to their endeavours, whereby they might be the better encouraged in their action.

176 In our assemblies at plays in London you shall see such heaving and shoving, such itching and shouldering, to sit by women—such care for their garments, that they be not trod on—such eyes to their laps, that no chips light in them—such pillows to their backs, that they take no hurt—such masking in their ears I know not what—such giving them pippins to pass the time—such playing at foot-saunt without cards —such ticking, such toying, such smiling, such winking and such manning them home when the sports are ended.

177 The theatre is your poet's Royal Exchange.

178 Silence much more in solemn state doth sit
In that fair concourse with an actor's voice
Than where rich Law insults, still vex'd with noise—
And where nine heralds could not crown her peace,
One Prologue here puts on her wreath with ease.

179   Give me that man
Can call the banish'd auditor home and tie
His ear with golden chains to his melody;
Can draw with adamantine pen even creatures
Forg'd out o' the hammer on tiptoe to reach up
And, from rare silence, clap their brawny hands
T'applaud what their charm'd soul scarce understands;
That man give me whose breast, fill'd by the muses
With raptures, into a second them infuses—
Can give an actor Sorrow, Rage, Joy, Passion,
Whilst he again, by self-same agitation,
Commands the hearers, sometimes drawing out tears,
Then smiles, and fills them both with hopes and fears.

180 'What is your profession?' said Roberto. 'Truly, sir,' said he, 'I am a player.' 'A player?'

175

quoth Roberto. 'I took you rather for a gentleman of great living, for, if by outward habit men
should be censured, I tell you you would be taken
for a substantial man.' 'So am I where I dwell,'
quoth the player, 'reputed able at my proper
cost to build a windmill. What though the world
once went hard with me, when I was fain to
carry my playing fardel a-footback? "Tempora
mutantur"—I know you know the meaning of it
better than I, but I thus conster it: "It's otherwise now"; for my very share in playing apparel
will not be sold for two hundred pounds.' 'Truly,'
said Roberto, ''Tis strange that you should so
prosper in that vain practice, for that it seems to
me your voice is nothing gracious.' 'Nay then,'
said the player, 'I mislike your judgment. Why,
I am as famous for Delphrigus and the King
of Fairies as ever was any of my time. The twelve
labours of Hercules have I terribly thundered on
the stage and played three scenes of the Devil in
the highway to Heaven.'

Proud as a player that feeds on the fruit of
divine poetry.

Sundry great disorders and inconveniencies
have been found to ensue to this city by the
inordinate haunting of great multitudes of people,
especially youth, to plays, interludes and shows
—namely, occasion of frays and quarrels; evil
practices of incontinency in great inns having
chambers and secret places adjoining to their
open stages and galleries; inveigling and alluring
of maids, specially orphans and good citizens'
children under age, to privy and unmeet contracts; the publishing of unchaste, uncomely and
unshamefast speeches and doings; withdrawing
of the Queen's Majesty's subjects from divine
service on Sundays and holidays, at which times
such plays were chiefly used; unthrifty waste of
the money of the poor and fond persons; sundry
robberies by picking and cutting of purses;
uttering of popular, busy and seditious matters;
and many other corruptions of youth and other
enormities—besides that also sundry slaughters
and mayhemings of the Queen's subjects have
happened by ruins of scaffolds, frames and stages,
and by engines, weapons and powder used in
plays.

The Plague

DEATH walked hand-in-hand with life during this age. Tempers were short and rapiers handy; diseases abounded and medical knowledge was primitive; a thousand doorways opened to the tomb. Above all, the terror of the plague hung over the country year by year; the joy of the spring was darkened by fears of what summer's hot days might bring.

Never completely absent, the plague rose at times to sudden fury. Hardly established as an actor and playwright, Shakespeare found himself, as a young man of twenty-eight, denied the opportunity of exercising his art for a period of two years, and, when he was at the height of his power, just at the time when Elizabeth finally succumbed, the plague once more closed the theatres, set the bells tolling dismally and emptied the city's streets. No doubt recent years have seen death's terrors descending upon London; but the proportion of citizens slain by the menace of the skies was but slight to the proportion of those who perished miserably of the creeping sickness, and while the sky's menace may be fought, against the plague no weapon availed. Men knew not whence it came and only dimly did they realize how it might be escaped. Always it formed the sombre background for the silks and the taffetas, the processions and the plays.

185 The purple whip of vengeance, the plague, having beaten many thousands of men, women and children to death, and still marking the people of this city every week by hundreds for the grave, is the only cause that all her inhabitants walk up and down like mourners at some great solemn funeral, the City herself being the chief mourners. The poison of this lingering infection strikes so deep into all men's hearts that their cheeks, like cowardly soldiers, have lost their colours; their eyes, as if they were in debt and durst not look abroad, do scarce peep out of their heads; and their tongues, like physicians ill-paid, give but cold comfort. By the power of their pestilent charms all merry meetings are cut off, all frolic assemblies dissolved, and in their circles are raised up the black, sullen and dogged spirits of sadness, of melancholy, and so, consequently, of mischief. Mirth is departed and lies dead and buried in men's bosoms; laughter dares not look a man in the face; jests are, like music to the deaf, not regarded; pleasure itself finds now no pleasure

but in sighing and bewailing the miseries of the time. For, alack! what string is there now to be played upon whose touch can make us merry? Playhouses stand like taverns that have cast out their masters, the doors locked up, the flags, like their bushes, taken down—or rather like houses lately infected, from whence the affrighted dwellers are fled, in hope to live better in the country.

What an unmatchable torment were it for a man to be barred up every night in a vast silent charnel-house—hung (to make it more hideous) with lamps dimly and slowly burning in hollow and glimmering corners; where all the pavement should, instead of green rushes, be strewed with blasted rosemary, withered hyacinths, fatal cypress and yew, thickly mingled with heaps of dead men's bones; the bare ribs of a father that begat him lying there, here the chapless hollow skull of a mother that bore him; round about him a thousand corses, some standing bolt upright in their knotted winding sheets, others half-mouldered in rotten coffins, that should suddenly yawn wide open, filling his nostrils with noisome stench and his eyes with the sight of nothing but crawling worms; and to keep such a poor wretch waking, he should hear no noise but of toads croaking, screech-owls howling, mandrakes shrieking! Were not this an infernal prison? Would not the strongest-hearted man (beset with such a ghastly horror) look wild, and run mad, and die?

And even such a formidable shape did the diseased city appear in. For he that durst (in the dead hour of gloomy midnight) have been so valiant as to have walked through the still and melancholy streets, what think you should have been his music? Surely the loud groans of raving sick men, the struggling pangs of souls departing —in every house grief striking up an alarm, servants crying out for masters, wives for husbands, parents for children, children for their mothers. Here he should have met some franticly running to knock up sextons; there, others fearfully sweating with coffins, to steal forth dead bodies lest the fatal handwriting of death should seal up their doors. And to make this dismal consort more full, round about him bells heavily tolling in one place and ringing out in another. The dreadfulness of such an hour is unutterable.

To arm the heart against this infection, when you have occasion to go forth of the house, having first eaten or drunken somewhat, you shall put into your mouth a clove or two, or a little cinnamon, or a piece of setwall, or of an orange peel, or, best of all, a piece of the root of angelica or elecampane, and take in your hand an orange, or a posy of rue or mint or balm, or else carry with you a handkerchief or sponge drenched in white vinegar of roses, if you can get it, if not, in common vinegar, especially white.

Take *Aloe Epaticum* or Cicotrine, fine cinnamon and Myrrh, of each of them three drams, Cloves, Mace, *Lignum Aloe*, Mastic, Bole Armeniac, of each of them half a dram; let all these things be well stamped in a clean mortar, then mingle them together, and after keep it in some close vessel, and take of it every morning two pennyweight in half a glass full of white wine with a little water and drink it in the morning at the dawning of the day. And so may you (by the grace of God) go hardly into all infection of the air and plague.

ORDERS TO BE SET DOWN BY THE LORD MAYOR AND ALDERMEN OF LONDON

Aldermen or their deputies

1. To give charge to Church-wardens, Constables, Parish Clerks, Sextons and Beadles to enquire what houses be infected.

2. To visit the ward often to see orders observed, especially touching cleanness in the streets.

3. The Aldermen or their deputies in their own persons to appoint Surveyors monthly in every parish.

4. To appoint that certificate may be made to them what houses be infected.

5. To give charge to all teachers of children that, as near as they can, they permit no children to come to their schools from infected houses,

especially till such houses have been clear by the space of twenty-eight days, and that none keep a greater number than their rooms shall be thought fit by the Alderman or their deputies to contain.

Surveyors

1. To see the orders for the sick executed daily and diligently upon knowledge from the Aldermen what houses be infected.

2. To appoint purveyors of necessaries for infected houses (being of the same houses) and deliver them red rods to carry, and see that none other resort to their houses.

Constables

1. To bring every day notice in writing to the Aldermen or their deputies what houses be infected.

Constable and Church-warden

1. To provide to have in readiness women to be providers and deliverers of necessaries to infected houses and to attend the infected persons, and they to bear red wands so that the sick may be kept from the whole as near as may be, needful attendance weighed.

Constable and Beadle

1. To enquire what houses be infected.

2. To view daily that papers remain upon doors twenty-eight days, or to place new.

Clerks and Sextons

1. To understand what houses be infected.

2. To see bills set upon the doors of houses infected.

3. To suffer no corpse infected to be buried or remain in the church during prayer or sermon, and to keep children from coming near them.

Scavengers and Rakers

1. To see the streets made clean every day, saving Sunday, and the soil to be carried away.

2. To warn all inhabitants against their houses to keep channels clear from filth (by only turning it aside), that the water may have passage.

Common Hunt

1. To kill dogs, &c. or to lose his place.

Householders and Houses

1. Houses having some sick though none die, or from whence some sick have been removed, are infected houses, and such are to be shut up for a month.

2. The whole family to tarry in twenty-eight days.

3. To keep shut the lower rooms for the like space.

4. One licensed to go for provision &c.

5. No clothes hanged into the streets.

6. Such as have wells or pumps, every morning by six and every evening after eight o'clock, shall cause ten buckets full to run into the streets.

7. Every evening at that hour the streets and channels to be made clean, the water not swept out of the channel, nor the streets over-wet but sprinkled &c.

8. The houses infected and things in them to be aired in the twenty-eight days, and no clothes or things about the infected persons to be given away or sold, but either destroyed or sufficiently purified.

9. Owners of houses infected, with their family, may within the month depart to any their houses in the country, or to any other house in the city, without being shut up, so they abstain from returning to the city, or from going abroad out of house in the city, for a month.

10. None shall keep dog or bitch abroad unled nor within howling or disturbing of their neighbours.

11. To have no assembly at funeral dinners or usual meeting in houses infected.

12. None shall for a month come into infected houses but such as be of the house and licensed to do service abroad.

13. No dunghills out of stables, bear-houses or other places to be made in the street.

14. To have double time of restraint for consenting to pull down bills, and the taker-away suffer imprisonment for eight days.

Two Viewers of dead bodies; Two Viewers of sick suspected—

Shall be appointed and sworn. These Viewers to report to the Constable, he to the Clerk, and he to the chief of Clerks upon pain of imprisonment. A pain of standing on the pillory for false reports by the Viewers. A loss of pension to such as shall refuse.

Mending of Pavements

That diligent care be had that pavements be amended where need is, and that principal paviers be appointed to survey the wants of paving, especially in channels, and that the dwellers against such may be forced to amend them.

Interludes and Plays

If the increase of the sickness be feared, that interludes and plays be restrained within the liberties of the city.

Physicians and Surgeons

That skilful and learned physicians and chirurgeons may be provided to minister to the sick.

Vagrant, Masterless and Poor People

1. That all such as be diseased be sent to St Thomas' or St Bartholomew's hospital, there to be first cured and made clean, and afterwards those which be not of the city to be sent away according to the statute in that case provided and the other to be set to work in such trades as are least used by the inhabitants of the city, for the avoiding of all such vagrant persons, as well children male and female, soldiers lame and maimed, as other idle and loitering persons that swarm in the streets and wander up and down begging, to the great danger and infecting of the city for the increase of the plague and annoyance to the same.

2. That all masterless men who live idly in the city without any lawful calling, frequenting places of common assemblies, as interludes, gaming-houses, cockpits, bowling alleys and such other places, may be banished the city.

Fair England

THE COUNTRYSIDE

THERE were still Forests of Arden in Elizabeth's time, and Gloucestershire wilds were ominous and terrifying. Outside of London no towns numbered more than a few thousand inhabitants; within their medieval walls their citizens still found space to live and work. Mile after long mile could be traversed without seeing human habitation, and even the more populated shires could show little more than scattered farms, shepherds' cottages and an occasional mansion set within fair demesnes.

The changes in country life most frequently noted by contemporaries were the enclosing of formerly tilled land for the pasturage of sheep, the consequent 'dearth' or dearness of farm produce and the throwing of many labourers out of employment, the gradual disappearance of limitless hospitality in the great houses and the penetration into the countryside of the newly rich. Perhaps some of the complaints were exaggerated, yet a change there definitely was, and the passage of the English scene was set towards its present miserable goal, where overpopulation eats up the arable land, the country content is ruined by the city and the sweetness of nature is polluted by human litter.

No action taken by Parliament could prevent the rise in prices. Elizabeth did her best by raising the standard of currency, severely debased during her father's reign, and for that she was lauded:

> Our current coin was metal base and mean
>   Till her most princely Grace the same put out
> By perfect gold and purèd silver clean,
>   Which pass for common coins her realms throughout:
> A deed deserving her perpetual praise,
> And public profit to this land always.

These coins, however, although they might pass for current, were hopelessly mixed with the older debased coins still in use, with foreign coins from France and Spain and the Low Countries, with moneys coined by individual merchants

—and confusion was further extended by the uncertain relationship between the values of the two essential metals, silver and gold. All of this was not the cause of the rise in prices but it certainly added to the Elizabethans' disturbance of mind over domestic economy and helped to direct attention towards what may be called the theme of gold.

190

191   Into the heart of England and Wales the muse here is entered—that is, Warwickshire, her native country.

192   O blessed life! pattern of that which our first parents led, the state of kings, now, being but a slavery to that of theirs. O school of contemplation! O thou picture of the whole world drawn in a little compass! O thou perspective glass, in whom we may behold upon earth all the frame and wonders of heaven! How happy, how thrice happy, is he that, not playing with his wings in the golden flames of the court, nor setting his foot into the busy throngs of the city, nor running up and down in the intricate mazes of the law, can be content in the winter to sit by a country fire, and the summer to lay his head on the green pillows of the earth, where his sleep shall be soft slumbers and his wakings pleasant as golden dreams.

Looking with more piercing eyes into the country life, I began to hate it worse than before I loved it: I fell to dispraise it faster than ever I did commend it. For I found it full of care and full of craft, full of labour and yet full of penury. I saw the poor husbandman made a slave to the rich farmer, the farmer racked by his landlord. I saw that covetousness made dear years when she had fullest barns, and to curse plenty for being liberal of her blessings. I had heard of no sin in the city but I met it in the village, nor any vice in the tradesman which was not in the ploughman.

Lord! how country folks can glose   193
    When they speak most untruly!
More craft was in a button'd cap
    And in an old wives' rail
Than in my life it was my hap
    To see on down or dale.
There was no open forgery,
    But underhanded gleaning—
Which they call country policy,
    But hath a worser meaning.

71

Some good bold-face bears out the wrong,
   Because he gains thereby;
The poor man's back is crack'd ere long,
   Yet there he lets him lie;
And no degree among them all
   But had such close intending
That I upon my knees did fall
   And pray'd for their amending.

195   There is no life more pleasant than a yeoman's life, but nowadays yeomanry is decayed, hospitality gone to wrack and husbandry almost quite fallen. The reason is because landlords, not contented with such revenues as their predecessors received, nor yet satisfied that they live like swinish epicures quietly at their ease, doing no good to the commonwealth, do leave no ground for tillage but do enclose for pasture many thousand acres of ground within one hedge, the husbandmen are thrust out of their own, or else by deceit constrained to sell all that they have.

196   You know the use and ancient custom of this realm of England was that all noblemen and gentlemen not called to attendance in our prince's service did continually inhabit the countries, continuing there from age to age, and from ancestor to ancestor, a continual house and hospitality—which got them great love among their neighbours, relieved many poor wretches and wrought also divers other good effects. But I see that gentlemen begin to take another course, and, falling from the use of their ancestors, do now either altogether (or very much) leave to dwell in their country houses, inhabiting cities and great towns, which manner of living I cannot allow.

The causes why hospitality is nowadays brought to so low a sail are five. The first is ambition, which moveth gentlemen that are of large revenues to wear gorgeous attires, to trail a costly port after them, to cavalier it abroad and, giving up house-keeping at home, to take a chamber in London, where they consume their time in viewing of stage-plays, in carousing of healths and, perhaps, in visiting of courtesans. The second is hatred, which pricketh gentlemen to fall out with their neighbours and to enrich the lawyers by commencing of suits and controversies. The third is covetousness, which persuadeth landlords to hoard up substance for the devil, to enhance incomes, to raise rents (for fear lest yeomen keep better hospitality than themselves) and to convert tillage into pastures. In consideration of which abominable abuse it was most prudently enacted in the last Parliament that all lands which were converted into sheep pastures or to the fatting or grazing of cattle (the same having been tillage lands) should be before the first of May in the year of our Lord 1599 last past restored to tillage by the possessors thereof and so should continue for ever. The fourth reason why hospitality is carried to so low an ebb proceedeth of building, for sooner shall we see a gentleman build a stately house than give alms and cherish the needy. The fifth and last cause of the decay of hospitality is gluttony, which induceth men to prepare artificial cookeries and divers sorts of meat, whereas one large and whole-

some mess of meat could peradventure counter-vail, yea, and go beyond all their junkets and dainty delicacies.

199 Where are the great chines of stalled beef? the great black-jacks of double beer? the long hall tables fully furnished with good victuals? and the multitude of good fellows assembling to the houses of potentates and men of worth? In a word, they are all banished with the spirit of the buttery; they are as rare in this age as common in former times. These potentates and gentlemen have begun in this manner to lessen their charge. First, for their three-years-stalled beef, it was too fat and triple charge; one year—nay, less—will serve to fat a bullock, the meat much sweeter and the charge much less. And so for other victuals of that kind. Now, for beef, mutton, veal, pig, goose and capon, which was the substance of their provision in those days, wherewith their tables were daily furnished, so that there was good cheer with plenty for them that sat, good reversions for them that waited, and great relief for the poor amongst those full platters—now, these bountiful and substantial dishes are changed into cates of less cost, though dishes of rarer device. Now there must be goose giblets, pigs' pettitoes and so many other boiled meats, forced meats and made dishes, as will supply the room of the substantial accustomed full platters to furnish the table, though they be but as cyphers in augrim to supply the number.

The stately lord, which wonted was to keep   200
A court at home, is now come up to court,
And leaves the country for a common prey,
To pilling, polling, bribing and deceit.

These young gallants, having lewdly spent   201
their patrimony, fall to begging of poor men's houses over their heads as the last refuge of their riot, removing the ancient bounds of lands to

73

support their decayed port, rather coveting to enclose that which was wont to be common than they would want to maintain their private prodigality.

202

203 I will tell you in one country where I came I saw a strange wonder: for, whereas in many other countries men did use to eat up the sheep, in that country sheep had eaten up both the men and their houses. For in the pastures, where I saw great flocks of sheep feeding, I might, near unto certain footpaths, behold here and there a piece of an old stone causeway which had been in times past some street or by-lane in some town or village, but now there was neither house nor town nor man left more than the shepherd and his sheepish master to look upon them.

204 Many farmhouses and villages wherein were maintained great numbers of people and by them the markets plentifully served with corn and other victuals, are now utterly decayed and put down for the feeding or grassing of beefs and muttons only. By means whereof the people which in such places were maintained are not only made vagrant, but also calves, hogs, pigs, geese, hens, chickens, capons, eggs, butter,

cheese and suchlike things do become exceedingly scarce and dear by want of their increase in those places, so that the markets are not, nor cannot be, served as in times past it hath been done.

205 There is not anything that belongs to housekeeping but it is a triple charge over it was; and whereas one hundred pounds a year was a competent living to maintain good hospitality, now three hundred pound a year will not defray the charge of such a house.

In times past I could have bought cloth for 2s. the broad yard, an hat for 12d., a shirt for 10d., a pair of boots for 2s., and whatsoever other necessaries belonged me at like rate. Now, I must pay three times dearer for any part of the said apparel.

206 Vorzooth, I am as honest a man's son as the best of them were, but vortune (Call you her a saint? Rather a devil) hath left me a beggar; and yet my vather a good yeoman, and lived many a winter's season in good repentation, and kept a homely house among his neighbours, and brought up his children cleanly so long as our old lease and landlord dured: but soothly, since they ended and that a merchant of the good town of Middlesex had dwelt among us a while, then varewell all our thrift; our sheep-shearing feasts, our beeves in harvest and the good pirrey in Christmas been all agone.

207 It is a world to see how most places of the realm are pestered with purveyors, who take up eggs, butter, cheese, pigs, capons, hens, chickens, hogs, bacon, etc. in one market under pretence of their commissions and suffer their wives to sell the same in another, or to poulterers of London. If these chapmen be absent but two or three market days then we may perfectly see these wares to be more reasonably sold, and thereunto the crosses sufficiently furnished of all things. In like sort, since the number of butter-men have so much increased, and since they travel in such wise that they come to men's

74

houses for their butter faster than they can make it, it is almost incredible to see how the price of butter is augmented; whereas when the owners were enforced to bring it to the market towns, and fewer of these butter-buyers were stirring, our butter was scarcely worth eighteen pence the gallon that now is worth three shillings fourpence and perhaps five shillings.

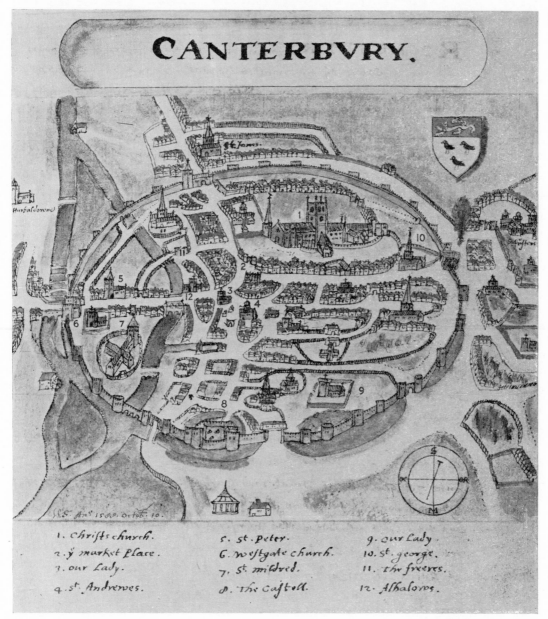

1. Chriſts church.
2. ÿ market place.
3. our Lady.
4. st. Andrewes.
5. st. peter.
6. weſtgate church.
7. st. mildred.
8. The caſtell.
9. our Lady.
10. st. george.
11. the freeres.
12. Alhalowes.

COUNTRY RECREATIONS

SINCE the countryside had but few entertainments save perhaps the occasional appearance of strolling actors or of itinerant ballad-singers, the scattered populace of the rural districts and the citizens of the small towns were induced to keep alive the many sports and pastimes they had inherited from their medieval progenitors. True, signs were not wanting that some of these recreations were moving towards oblivion, but up to the end of Elizabeth's reign the May games, the morris dancings and their associated festivities remained vital in the lives of the people.

For the gentlemen and their ladies, hunting provided most amusement—whether the coursing of hares, the chasing of the stag or the still more characteristic art of falconry. Contemporary literature is so full of current allusions to these entertainments that we can remain in no doubt concerning their almost universal appeal. No man who professed gentility could neglect a detailed knowledge of hunting and its terms; no countryman, however humble, was without an interest in these sports of the nobility.

At our meetings on the holidays between our lads and the wenches, such true mirth at honest meetings, such dancing on the green, in the market-house or about the maypole, where the young folks smiling kiss at every turning and the old folks checking with laughing at their children when dancing for the garland, playing at stoolball for a tansy and a banquet of curds and cream, with a cup of old nappy ale, matter of small charge, with a little reward of the piper, after casting of sheep's eyes, and faith and troth for a bargain; clapping of hands are seals to the truth of hearts, when a pair of gloves and a handkerchief are as good as the best obligation, with a cap and a curtsy, hie ye home, maids, to milking—and so merrily goes the day away.

at home (as seldom we are) and with them we play at dice and cards, sorting ourselves according to the number of players and their skill, some to Tick-Tack, some Lurch, some to Irish Game or Doublets: other sit close to the cards at Post-and-Pair, at Ruff, or Colchester Trump, at Mack or Maw; yea, there are some ever so fresh gamesters, as will bear you company at Novem Quinque, at Faring, Treytrip or One-and-Thirty. And in winter nights we use certain Christmas games very proper and of much agility. We want not also pleasant mad-headed knaves, that be properly learned and will read in divers pleasant books and good authors, as *Sir Guy of Warwick*, *The Four Sons of Aymon*, *The Ship of Fools*, *The Budget of Demands*, *The Hundreth Merry Tales*, *The Book of Riddles*, and many other excellent writers, both witty and pleasant.

In fair weather, when we have strangers or holidays (for else in the day time we attend our thrift), we exercise ourselves in shooting at butts, pricks, rovers and rownes; we cast the bar or sledge, leap or run, if our ages and condition be fit for such exercise, else, being aged, we chat at home and talk of Thérouanne and Tournai or some other notable war wherein we served our prince.

In foul weather we send for some honest neighbours, if happily we be with our wives alone

214

215 Man, I dare challenge thee to throw the sledge,
To jump or leap over a ditch or hedge,
To wrastle, play a stoolball, or to run,
To pitch the bar, or to shoot off a gun,
To play at loggats, nine-holes or ten-pins,
To try it out at football by the shins—
At tick-tack, Irish, noddy, maw and ruff,
At hot-cockles, leap-frog or blindman-buff,
To drink half pots or deal at the whole can,
To play at base or 'pen-and-inkhorn, Sir Jhan',
To dance the morris, play at barley-break,
At all exploits a man can think or speak,
At shove-groat, venture-point or cross-and-pile,
At 'beshrew him that's last at yonder stile',
At leaping o'er a midsummer bonfire
Or at the 'drawing-dun-out-of-the-mire'.

216   Dost thou love hawking?

Why, you know an a man have not skill in the 217
hawking and hunting languages nowadays, I'll
not give a rush for him: they are more studied
than the Greek or the Latin. He is for no gallant's
company without 'hem.

What sense so sad, what mind so maz'd, but sets 218
his sorrows by
When once the falcon free begins to scud amid
the sky,
To turn and wind a bird by sleight, and eke at
last to slay,
With strong encounter, doves and ducks and
every other prey—
The pretty partridge, rails and quails that haunt
the open field,
And from her mountee to enforce the heron
haught to yield
By binding with her close in clouds, in manner
out of sight—
For noble peers and chiefest states a passing
pleasant flight.
So small a bird, so large a fowl at such a lofty gate
To reach and rap and force to fall, it is a game of
state.

Or, if you had rather have some music to 219
content your ear, out goes our dogs—our
hounds, I should have said; with them we
make a heavenly noise or cry that would make
a dead man revive and run on foot to hear it.

A DITTY OF HUNTING, TO THE TUNE   220
OF LIGHT-OF-LOVE, ETC.

Of all the pleasures in country and court
Hunting with hounds is the gallantest sport.
Though painful it seemeth, yet health it doth
bring:
It is a pastime for a duke or a king.
    Merrily chants the hounds in the wood:
    Most men it delights, the noise is so good.

Consider, I pray, their great trouble and 221
pains. Such violent labour, such dangerous
riding, the highways cannot always contain them,
but over the hedges and ditches. Here begins
the cry and the curse of the poor tenant, who sits

78

at a hard rent and sees his corn spoiled. Then immediately follows the renting of garments, the tearing of flesh, the breaking of legs, the cracking of bones—their lives are not always secured. And thus they continue the whole day, sometimes through storms and tempests, sometimes enforced to wade through rivers and brooks, fasting, sweating and wearied only with a conceit of their booty (here is excellent sport indeed). If they were to be hired, they would never undertake such troublesome and dangerous courses; then it would seem to be a mere slavery, as indeed it doth to their servants and followers, who must attend their lordships and partake with them in their whole sport, but not in any part of their pleasure. In truth, according to right reason, I should prefer the life of a carrier or a post far before theirs.

THE ROADS AND THE INNS

TRAVELLING in sixteenth-century England was by way of being both an adventure and a trial. The roads were excessively bad, in places mere tracks across desert land, at the best heavily rutted and, when the rains fell, knee-deep in mud. Perhaps the most comfortable means of getting from one place to another was by merrily jogging the foot-path way; for those who had to make more rapid journeys or for whom honour demanded a more dignified manner of travel the horse alone was available. Carts might convey possessions, and ladies might make use of them in pilgrimage, but except for a restricted area round London the wheeled carriage was but of little use.

To remedy matters somewhat, there was an efficient service of post-horses and nearly all accounts give pleasant praise to the wayside inns. There was careful attention to travellers' needs and the food was agreeable. It is true that certain ostlers gained an evil reputation because of their association with the highway robbers; but such incidental dangers were taken in their stride by the Elizabethans. Every traveller carried his weapon of defence; even clergymen, if they elected not to avail themselves of a pistol, went with sword at side and dagger in belt.

222 Coaches are not to be hired anywhere but only at London; and howsoever England is for the most part plain, or consisting of little pleasant hills, yet the ways far from London are so dirty as hired coachmen do not ordinarily take any long journeys, but only for one or two days any way from London, the ways so far being sandy and very fair and continually kept so by labour of hands. And for a day's journey a coach with two horses used to be let for some ten shillings the day (or, the way being short, for some eight shillings, so as the passengers paid for the horses' meat) or some fifteen shillings a day for three horses, the coachman paying for his horses' meat.

For the most part Englishmen, especially in long journeys, use to ride upon their own horses. But if any will hire a horse, at London they use to pay two shillings the first day and twelve, or perhaps eighteen pence, a day for as many days as they keep him till the horse be brought home to the owner, and the passenger must either bring him back or pay for the sending of him, and find him meat both going and coming. In other parts of England a man may hire a horse for twelve pence the day, finding him meat and bringing or sending him back; and, if the journey be long, he may hire him at a convenient rate for a month or two. Likewise carriers let horses from city to city, with caution that the passenger must lodge in their inn, that they may look to the feeding of their horse, and so they will for some five or six days' journey let him a horse and find the horse meat themselves for some twenty shillings. Lastly, these carriers have long covered wagons in which they carry passengers from city to city; but this kind of journeying is so tedious, by reason they must take wagon very early and come very late to their inns, as none but women and people of inferior condition, or strangers (as Flemings with their wives and servants) use to travel in this sort.

223   Faith, I have had a foolish odd mischance that angers me. Coming over Shooter's Hill, there came a fellow to me like a sailor and asked me money; and whilst I stayed my horse to draw my purse, he takes th' advantage of a little bank and leaps behind me, whips my purse away, and, with a sudden jerk I know not how, threw me at least three yards out of my saddle. I never was so robbed in all my life.

224   I might here speak of the excessive staves which divers that travel by the way do carry upon their shoulders, whereof some are twelve or thirteen foot long, beside the pike of twelve inches; but, as they are commonly suspected of honest men to be thieves and robbers, or at the leastwise scarce true men which bear them, so by reason of this and the like suspicious weapons the honest traveller is now enforced to ride with a case of dags at his saddle-bow, or with some pretty short snapper, whereby he may deal with them further off in his own defence before he come within the danger of these weapons.

Finally, no man travelleth by the way without his sword or some such weapon with us, except the minister, who commonly weareth none at all, unless it be a dagger or hanger at his side.

Seldom also are they or any other wayfaring men robbed without the consent of the chamberlain, tapster or ostler where they bait and lie, who, feeling at their alighting whether their capcases or budgets be of any weight or not, by taking them down from their saddles, or otherwise see their store in drawing of their purses, do by-and-by give intimation to some one or other attendant daily in the yard or house, or dwelling hard by, upon such matches whether the prey be worth the following or no.

There is no place in the world where passengers 225 may so freely command as in the English inns, and are attended for themselves and their horses as well as if they were at home, and perhaps better, each servant being ready at call in hope of a small reward in the morning.

As soon as a passenger comes to an inn, the 226 servants run to him, and one takes his horse and walks him till he be cold, then rubs him and gives him meat—yet I must say that they are not much to be trusted in this last point without the eye of the master or his servant to oversee them. Another servant gives the passenger his private chamber and kindles his fire; the third pulls off his boots and makes them clean. Then the host or hostess visits him, and if he will eat with the host or at a common table with others, his meal will cost him six pence, or in some places but four pence (yet this course is less honourable and not used by gentlemen); but if he will eat in his chamber, he commands what meat he will according to his appetite and as much as he thinks fit for him and his company—yea, the kitchen is open to him to command the meat to be dressed as he best likes; and when he sits at table, the host or hostess will accompany him, or, if they have many guests, will at least visit him, taking it for courtesy to be bid sit down. While he eats, if he have company especially, he shall be offered music, which he may freely take or refuse, and, if he be solitary, the musicians will give him the good day with music in the morning. It is the custom and no way disgraceful to set up part of supper for his breakfast. In the evening or in the morning after breakfast (for the common sort use not to dine but ride from breakfast to supper-time, yet coming early to the inn for better resting of their horses), he shall have a reckoning in writing, and, if it seem unreasonable, the host will satisfy him either for the due price or by abating part, especially if the servant deceive him any way, which one of experience will soon find. A man cannot more freely command at home in his own house than he may do in his inn, and at parting, if he give some few pence to the chamber-lain and ostler, they wish him a happy journey.

27 One that eats alone in his own chamber with one or two servants attending him perhaps upon reckoning may spend some five or six shillings for supper and breakfast.

28 The neat cleanliness, the exquisite fineness, the pleasant and delightful furniture in every point for household, wonderfully rejoiced me; their chambers and parlours strewed over with sweet herbs refreshed me; their nosegays finely intermingled with sundry sorts of fragrant flowers in their bedchambers and privy rooms, with comfortable smell cheered me up and entirely delighted all my senses.

I would fain go to sleep. 229
'Let us go.'
Show me the privies.
'They be at your chamber: smell it.'
O how he stinketh!
'Mark! It passeth a gillyflower in scent.'
Let us go hence. O mischief!

HOW TO KILL FLEAS DIVERS WAYS 230

First, to gather all the fleas of thy chamber into one place, anoint a staff with the grease of a fox or hedgehog, and lay the staff again where you list in your chamber, and it shall so gather all the fleas by it. Also fill a dish with goat's blood and set the same by the bed, and all the fleas will come to it round about. And the like will they do by the blood of the hedgehog. Also take the fat of a goat and anoint what you list therewith, and set the same under your bed, and all the fleas will gather unto the same. Also take lupines or flat beans and boil them in water with wormwood, and that water sprinkle well about the chamber, and all the fleas shall avoid that chamber. Also take an apple of coloquintida and infuse the same in water, and in that water boil wormwood, which, cast about the chamber, killeth all the fleas. And the like doth the peach leaves, or vervain, or coliander boiled in water, and so cast about.

Or, taking them betwixt your nails, you may 231 bruise them at your pleasure.

THE ROGUES AND VAGABONDS

IN the year 1596 the Venetian Francesco Gradenigo, after praising England as the most lovely country imaginable, declared that 'poverty hath no place there'. 'Personally', he says, 'I have not seen a beggar yet.'

It would be pleasant to believe his observation correct, but facts will not permit endorsement of this roseate report. During Elizabeth's reign much was done to relieve the worthy poor; at the same time the tribe of Autolycus was legion. Ragged rogues haunted the countryside and rogues in satin plagued the towns. Even if we are prepared to deem some of the pamphleteers' statements a trifle exaggerated, we cannot escape the records of the time. Vagabondage, induced by a series of social changes, was a real and potent problem both for the authorities in London and for the ordinary citizen.

These vagabonds exercised their quality from the filching of linen off wayside hedges to the pursuit of highway robbery. They had their own social distinctions and to a large extent their own language. In effect, they formed a community within a community, and no efforts of the justices were sufficient to curb their nefarious activities. For us they are a picturesque part of Elizabethan life, but for contemporaries they seemed a continual nuisance and at times a worrying menace.

232   Beggers Bush.   A Maundering Begger.   A gallant Begger.

233 As of ancient and long time there hath been, and is now at this present, many good, godly, profitable laws and acts made and set forth in this most noble and flourishing realm for the relief, succour, comfort and sustentation of the poor, needy, impotent and miserable creatures being and inhabiting in all parts of the same, so is there most wholesome estatutes, ordinances and necessary laws made, set forth and published for the extreme punishment of all vagrants and sturdy vagabonds as passeth through and by all parts of this famous isle, most idly and wickedly.

All these rowsy, ragged rabblement of rakehells.

Villains they are by birth, varlets by education, knaves by profession, beggars by the statute and rogues by Act of Parliament. They are the idle drones of a country, the caterpillars of a commonwealth and the Egyptian lice of a kingdom.

It was necessary that a people so fast increasing and so daily practising new and strange villainies should borrow to themselves a speech which, so near as they could, none but themselves should understand; and for that cause was this language, which some call 'Pedlar's French', invented, to th' intent that, albeit any spies should secretly steal into their companies to discover them, they might freely utter their minds one to another, yet avoid the danger. The language, therefore, of *canting* they study even from their infancy, that is to say from the very first hour that they take upon them the names of 'kinchin coes', till they are grown 'rufflers' or 'upright men', which are the highest in degree amongst them.

A Ruffler goeth with a weapon to seek service, saying he hath been a servitor in the wars, and beggeth for his relief. But his chiefest trade is to rob poor wayfaring men and market-women.

A Prigman goeth with a stick in his hand like an idle person. His property is to steal clothes off the hedge, which they call 'storing of the rogueman'.

A Whipjack is one that, by colour of a counterfeit licence (which they call a 'gibe', and the seals they call 'jarks'), doth use to beg like a mariner; but his chiefest trade is to rob booths in a fair, or to pilfer ware from stalls, which they call 'heaving of the booth'.

A Frater goeth with a like licence to beg for some spittal-house or hospital. Their prey is commonly upon poor women as they go and come to the markets.

A Quire Bird is one that came lately out of prison, and goeth to seek service. He is commonly a stealer of horses, which they term a 'prigger of palfreys'.

An Upright Man is one that goeth with the truncheon of a staff, which staff they call a 'filchman'. This man is of so much authority that, meeting with any of his profession, he may call them to account and command a share or 'snap' unto himself of all that they have gained by their trade in one month. And if he do them wrong, they have no remedy against him—no, though he beat them, as he useth commonly to do. He may also command any of their women, which they call 'doxies', to serve his turn. He hath the chief place at any market walk and other assemblies, and is not of any to be controlled.

I once took one of them into my service, being a sturdy, big-limbed young fellow. Of him I desired some knowledge in their gibberish, but he swore he could not cant—yet his rogueship, seeing himself used kindly by me, would now and then shoot out a word of canting, and being thereupon asked why with oaths he denied it before, he told me that they are sworn never to disclose their skill in canting to any householder, for, if they do, the other 'maunderers' or rogues 'mill' them (kill them), yet he for his part, he said, was never sworn, because he was a 'clapperdudgeon', that is to say, a beggar born. This 'clapperdudgeon' stayed with me so long as he durst, and then 'binged a waste in a darkmans' (stole away from me in the night-time).

Let my pen gallop over a few lines, and it shall bring you, without spurring, swiftlier into Gloucestershire than if you rode upon Pacolet. There if you please to alight near Tewkesbury, at a place called Durrest Fair (being kept there upon the two Holy Rood days), you shall see more rogues than ever were whipped at a cart's arse through London, and more beggars than ever came dropping out of Ireland. If you look upon them, you would think you lived in Henry the Sixth's time, and that Jack Cade and his rebellious ragamuffins were there mustering. And these swarms of locusts come to this lousy fair from all parts of the land within an hundred miles' compass. To describe the booths is lost labour, for, let the hangman show but his wardrobe, and there is not a rag difference between them. None here stands crying, 'What do you

238

239

lack?' for you can ask for nothing that is good but here it is lacking. The buyers and sellers are both alike, tawny sun-burned rascals, and they flock in such troops that it shows as if Hell were broke loose. The shopkeepers are thieves and the chapmen rogues, beggars and whores; so that to bring a purse-full of money hither were madness, for it is sure to be cut.

But would you know what wares these merchants of eel-skins utter? Only 'duds for the quarroms', that is to say, clothes for the body, which they have pilfered from hedges or houses. And this filthy fair begins before day and endeth before nine in the same morning. At which breaking up, they do not presently march away with their bags and their baggages, but he who is chosen the Lord of the Fair, who is commonly the lustiest rogue in the whole bunch, leads his tattered footmen and footwomen from ale-house to ale-house, where, being armed all in ale-of-proof, and their 'bene bouse' (the strong liquor) causing them to have 'nase nabs' (drunken coxcombs), up fling they the cans, down go the booths, about fly broken jugs. Here lies a rogue bleeding, there is a 'mort' cursing, here a 'doxy' stabbing with her knife. And thus this fair, which begins merrily, ends madly; for knaves set it up and queans pull it down.

WITCHES AND FAIRIES

THE Elizabethan world was populated with many mysterious beings. No doubt the more sceptical were prepared to reject the idea of fairies dancing in the moonlight and performing their kindly services to good milkmaids or punishing the sluttish, but the pressure of folk legend was too great and too immediate to permit of complete disbelief. A smile may have been on the faces of many as they spoke of Robin Goodfellow, yet, in view of the numerous supposed magical wonders of nature, hardly one of them could be absolutely sure. A world which included the unicorn and the phoenix could readily accommodate the race of fairies.

Many characteristics of these fairies were benevolent, but fear mixed with wonder when men thought of them. Holinshed's well-known account of the prophecies given on the blasted heath to Macbeth and Banquo declares 'the common opinion that these women were either the weird sisters, that is (as ye would say) the goddesses of destiny, or else some nymphs or fairies'; and Reginald Scot avers that certain wicked women, 'seduced by the illusion of devils', 'profess that in the night-times they ride abroad with Diana or else with Herodias, and do whatsoever those fairies or ladies command'. With witches, then, the fairies were at least sometimes associated, and concerning the reality of witchcraft there were but few in the age so bold as to utter disbelief. The countryside was hag-ridden and, although the witch-hunt did not attain its full ferocity until the accession of James, the reign of Elizabeth saw quite enough of arrests and burnings. The force of the spell was as potent for Shakespeare's contemporaries as any tangible force of nature.

84

Another sort there be, that will
Be talking of the fairies still,
Nor never can they have their fill,
   As they were wedded to them:
No tales of them their thirst can slake,
So much delight therein they take,
And some strange thing they fain would make,
   Knew they the way to do them.

In our childhood our mothers' maids have so terrified us with an ugly devil having horns on his head, fire in his mouth, and a tail in his breech, eyes like a basin, fangs like a dog, claws like a bear, a skin like a niger and a voice roaring like a lion, whereby we start and are afraid when we hear one cry 'Bough'; and they have so fraied us with bull-beggars, spirits, witches, urchins, elves, hags, fairies, satyrs, pans, fauns, silens, kit-with-the-canstick, tritons, centaurs, dwarfs, giants, imps, calcars, conjurors, nymphs, changelings, incubus, Robin Goodfellow, the spoorn, the mare, the man-in-the-oak, the hell-wain, the firedrake, the puckle, Tom Thumb, hob-goblin, Tom Tumbler, Boneless, and such other bugs, that we are afraid of our own shadows.

Know you this by the way, that heretofore Robin Goodfellow and Hobgoblin were as terrible, and also as credible to the people, as hags and witches be now.

Many witches are found there, who frequently do much mischief by means of hail and tempests.

There be two or three in our town which I like not, but especially an old woman. I have been as careful to please her as ever I was to please mine own mother, and to give her ever anon one thing or other; and yet methinks she frowns at me now and then. And I had a hog which ate his meat with his fellows and was very well to our thinking over night, and in the morning he was stark dead. My wife hath had five or six hens even of late dead. Some of my neighbours wish me to burn something alive, as a hen or a hog. Others will me in time to seek help at the hands of some cunning man, before I have any further harm. I would be glad to do for the best. 246

247

The Home

HOUSES AND GARDENS

FAMILIARLY, we apply the term 'Elizabethan' to all those black-and-white timbered cottages and farms which may still be found scattered widely over the English countryside. Many of them do not fall strictly within the period 1558–1603; some are of fifteenth-century structure, numerous others belong to the seventeenth century; but the term 'Elizabethan' is as good as any for designating a type of building which, inherited from medieval days, provided an almost unaltering pattern for yeomen and burgesses during this long reign. The Hathaway farm at Shottery and the Shakespeare house in Stratford are alike in general formation. The only characteristic Elizabethan development lay in the increasing tendency to carve timbers which in the past would have remained rudely planed by the adze and in the more elaborate moulding of ceilings.

If the yeomen and the ordinary citizens were content with traditional forms, however, the nobility and the recently rich sought outward expression of their wealthy state in the erection of mansions of newer style. Some were satisfied with the enlargement of their existing timbered dwellings, but numerous others sought to fashion in stone houses of an entirely new sort. Italian influence brought in classical pillars; walls were broken to allow of great windows, which some critics severely condemned; ornately carved staircases gave a sense of splendour and dignity; new types of rooms came rapidly into being; from the

86

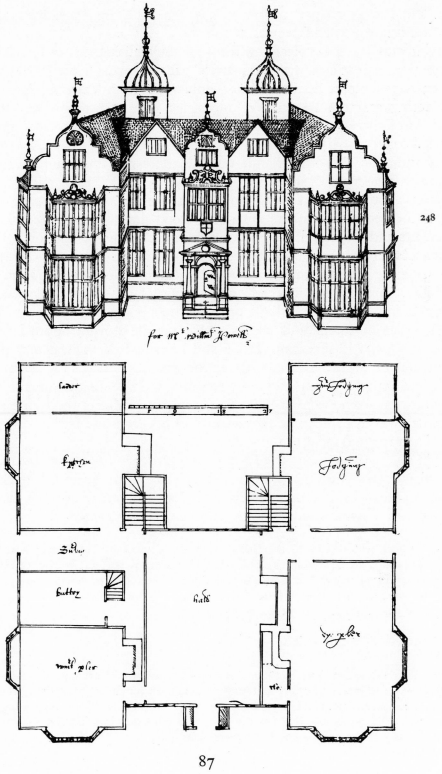

for Mr. willm Howeth

248

87

roofs fantastically shaped chimneys rose like clustered gargoyles stretching their necks upwards and peering at the sky.

Architecturally, the typical new form for the mansion was an H or E; and, in the interior, a great hall, with a minstrels' gallery, together with a 'long gallery' on the second floor, became almost universal. Mantlepieces heavily carved, wainscoting and the free use of tapestries gave the rooms an appearance symbolic of the age, the rich gold and silver embroidery set off against the panelled oak.

Furniture, on the other hand, was generally not dominant in any room. Carved chests served both as useful receptacles and as seats; joint-stools were common; a few heavy chairs and tables in the living rooms and great four-poster beds in the sleeping chambers sometimes stood almost in majestic isolation. As ornaments and for utilitarian purposes gold and silver vessels (or, in humbler homes, pewter) glittered and glowed against the even-toned woodwork.

Outside the mansions, gardens were beginning to assume importance. New and hitherto unknown plants came into ordinary fame, and ingenious souls took delight in imposing formal shape upon nature's profusion. Whatever the novel joy, however, in 'knots' and 'mazes', whatever the growing appreciation of the flower beds, the Elizabethan garden still remained of chiefest service for the production of herbs. Herbs both in the kitchen and the sickroom were of sovereign import. It was not only hermits and the English counterparts of Friar Lawrence who were deep in their lore; knowledge of their virtues, real or imagined, was of paramount significance for all, from the farmer to the nobleman, from the milkmaid to the Queen.

As in other affairs of life, the Elizabethan gardener was constrained to govern his actions by the heavens, and the present-day rustic belief in the potency of the moon seems as nothing compared with such sixteenth-century instructions as appear in Thomas Hill's *The proffitable arte of gardening*:

249   When Saturn and the Moon are either threescore degrees of the Zodiac asunder (which distance is called a sextile aspect), or when they are asunder 120 degrees (which is called a triangle, trigone or tryent aspect), then is it good to labour the earth, for either sowing, tilling, gardening, vining or building. But when they are a quarter of the Zodiac asunder (called a quartel aspect, which is 90 degrees), then meddle not in such matters.

Here, too, the planets ruled.

250   Houses are built to live in and not to look on: therefore let use be preferred before uniformity, except where both may be had. Leave the goodly fabrics of houses, for beauty only, to the enchanted palaces of the poets—who build them with small cost. He that builds a fair house upon an ill seat commiteth himself to prison. Neither do I reckon it an ill seat only where the air is unwholesome, but likewise where the air is unequal.

88

254

251   Order and edify the house so that the principal and chief prospects may be East and West, specially North-east, South-east and South-west, for the meridial wind of all winds is the most worst, for the South wind doth corrupt and doth make evil vapours. The East wind is temperate, frisk and fragrant, the West wind mutable, the North wind purgeth evil vapours; wherefore better it is of the two worst that the windows do open plain North than plain South.

252   There are old men yet dwelling in the village where I remain which have noted three things to be marvellously altered in England within their sound remembrance.

One is the multitude of chimneys lately erected.

253   The bricklayer hath this policy—when he maketh a stately place all glorious to the eye and full of fair chambers and goodly rooms, and about the house perhaps some threescore chimneys, yet he can so cunningly cast by his art that three of them shall not smoke in the twelve month, and so spoils he much good mortar and brick.

'Why,' quoth I, 'the fault is not in the workman but the housekeeper; for nowadays men build for to please the eye, not to profit the poor. They use no rest but for themselves and their household, nor no fire but in a little court chimney in their own chamber. How can the poor bricklayer then be blamed, when the niggardness of the lord or master is the cause no more chimneys do smoke? For would they use ancient hospitality as their forefathers did, and value as lightly of pride as their great-grandfathers, then should you see every chimney in the house smoke, and prove that the poor artificer had done his part.'

255   Painted chimnies in great country houses make a show afar off and catch travellers' eyes; but coming near them, neither cast they smoke, nor hath the house the heart to make you drink.

256   The walls of our houses on the inner sides be either hanged with tapestry, arras work or painted cloths, wherein either divers histories, or herbs, beasts, knots and such like are stained, or else they are sealed with oak of our own, or wainscot brought hither out of the east countries, whereby the rooms are not a little commended, made warm and much more close than otherwise they would be.

257

258

The furniture of our houses also exceedeth and 259
is grown in manner even to passing delicacy:
and herein I do not speak of the nobility and
gentry only, but likewise of the lowest sort in
most places of our south country that have anything at all to take to. Certes in noblemen's
houses it is not rare to see abundance of arras,
rich hangings of tapestry, silver vessel and so
much other plate as may furnish sundry cupboards to the sum oftentimes of a thousand or
two thousand pounds at the least, whereby the
value of this and the rest of their stuff doth grow
to be almost inestimable. Likewise in the houses
of knights, gentlemen, merchantmen and some
other wealthy citizens it is not geson to behold
generally their great provision of tapestry,
Turkey work, pewter, brass, fine linen and thereto costly cupboards of plate, worth five or six

hundred or a thousand pounds to be deemed by estimation. Even the inferior artificers and many farmers have, for the most part, learned also to garnish their cupboards with plate, their joined beds with tapestry and silk hangings, and their tables with carpets and fine napery, whereby the wealth of our country (God be praised therefor, and give us grace to employ it well) doth infinitely appear.

261 Our fathers, yea and we ourselves also, have lain full oft upon straw pallets, on rough mats covered only with a sheet, under coverlets made of dagswain or hop-harlots (I use their own terms), and a good round log under their heads instead of a bolster or pillow.

263

264

265

266

THE BEST BED-CHAMBER

In the best bed-chamber, seven pieces of hangings of embroidery of cloth of gold and silver, cloth of tissue, velvet of sundry colours and needle-work, twelve foot deep—one piece of the picture of Faith and his contrary Mahomet, another piece with the picture of Hope and the contrary Judas, another piece with the picture of Temperance and the contrary Sardanapalus, the other four pieces paned and wrought with flowers and slips of needle-work; a bedstead gilt; a fair large sparver and bedstead with double valance of cloth of gold, cloth of silver, sundry colours of velvet, embroidered fair with divers arms, with portals and pictures, and with a deep gold fringe; six curtains of blue and red satin, striped with gold and silver and laid with gold lace about the edges and a gold twist down the seams, and fringed about with gold fringe; a matress; a down bed; a down bolster; two pillows; a wool quilt; a pair of fustians; a white Spanish rug; a counterpoint of cloth of tissue paned with cloth of gold and silver and a broad gold lace and gold fringe about it, lined with crimson sarcenet; a purple sarcenet quilt; three foot Turkey carpets, the ground of them white, to lay about the bed; a square table inlaid; a carpet for it of needle-work, made with a rose and antiques with a broad gold and silver lace, with a border of white satin

268

embroidered and a gold fringe; a cupboard; a carpet for it of the story of David and Nathan, with trees, of needle-work, and a border of crimson velvet about it and gold fringe; a great chair trimmed with crimson velvet embroidered with gold and with a gold fringe; another little chair and a little stool suitable, with a gold fringe; a little stool covered with crimson velvet embroidered with needle-work flowers; two French stools inlaid set with marble stones; a joint-stool; two needle-work cushions for the windows, whereof one with my Lord and my Lady's arms wrought in it and lined with crimson satin, the other of Europa wrought with silk, gold and silver, and lined with China cloth of gold; a cushion for the chair of crimson velvet embroidered with pearl, with gold fringe about, with tassels of silver and yellow silk and lined with cloth of silver; a screen with a cover for it of carnation velvet embroidered with gold and a gold fringe; a little desk of mother-of-pearl; a fair pair of copper andirons; a fire-shovel; a pair of tongs; a close-stool covered with leather; a stool pan; a chamberpot; wainscot under the windows.

271

269   The third thing they tell of is the exchange of vessel, as of treen platters into pewter and wooden spoons into silver or tin.

270

He must be an unskilled farmer who does not 272 possess gilt silver salt-cellars, silver cups and spoons.

It is a world to see in these our days, wherein 273 gold and silver most aboundeth, how that our gentility, as loathing those metals because of the plenty, do now generally choose rather the Venice glasses, both for our wine and beer, than any of those metals or stone wherein beforetime we have been accustomed to drink. And as this is seen in the gentility, so in the wealthy communalty the like desire of glass is not neglected. The poorest also will have glass if they may, but, sith the Venetian is somewhat too dear for them, they content themselves with such as are made at home of fern and burned stone.

Among the better sort of gentlemen and merchants few are found who have not cupboards of silver and gold plate to the value of two hundred pounds at the least.

275 If you look into our gardens annexed to our houses, how wonderfully is their beauty increased, not only with flowers and variety of curious and costly workmanship, but also with rare and medicinable herbs sought up in the land within these forty years—so that, in comparison of this present, the ancient gardens were but dunghills and laistowes to such as did possess them. How art also helpeth nature in the daily colouring, doubling and enlarging the proportion of our flowers, it is incredible to report: for so curious and cunning are our gardeners now in these days that they presume to do in manner what they list with nature and moderate her course in things as if they were her superiors.

277

Morsus Diaboli.
Diuels bit.

✳ *The description.*

Diuels bit hath small vpright rounde stalkes of a cubite high, beset with long leaues somewhat broade, very little or nothing snipt about the edges, somewhat hairie and euen. The flowers are of a darke purple colour, fashioned like the flowers of Scabious, which being ripe are caried away with the winde. The root is black, thicke, harde, & short, with many threddie strings fastned thereto. The great part of the roote seemeth to be bitten away; old fantasticke charmers report, that the diuell did bite it for enuie, bicause it is an herbe that hath so many good vertues, and is so beneficiall to mankinde.

✳ *The place.*

Diuels bit groweth in drie medowes & woods, and about waies sides. I haue founde great store of it growing in Hampsteede woode neere London, at Lee in Essex, and at Raleigh in Essex, in a woode called Hammerell, and sundrie other places.

✳ *The time.*

It flowreth in August, and is harde to be known from Scabious, sauing when it flowreth.

✳ *The names.*

It is commonly called *Morsus Diaboli*, or Diuels bit, of the root (as it seemeth) that is bitten off. For the superstitious people hold opinion, that the diuell for the enuie that he beareth to mankind bit it off, bicause it woulde be otherwise good for many vses: it is called of *Fuchsius Succisa*: in high **Teuffels abbiß**: in lowe Dutch **Duvuelles beet**: in French *Mors du Diable*: in English Diuels bit, and Fore bit.

✳ *The temperature.*

Diuels bit is something bitter, and of a hot and drie temperature, and that in the latter end of the second degree.

✳ *The vertues.*

There is no better thing against old swellings of the almonds, and vpper parts of the throte that A be hardly ripened.

It clenseth away slimie flegme that sticketh in the iawes, it digesteth and consumeth it : and it B quicklie taketh away the swellings in those partes, if the decoction thereof be often helde in the mouth and gargarized, especially if a little quantitie of *Mel Rosarum*, or honie of Roses be put into it.

It is reported to be good for all the infirmities that Scabious serueth for, and to be of no lesse C force against the stingings of venemous beasts, poisons, and pestilent diseases, and to consume and waste away plague sores, being stamped and laide vpon them.

And also to mitigate the paines of the matrix or mother, and to driue foorth winde if the decoc- D tion thereof be drunke.

278

Of

LOVE, MARRIAGE AND CHILDREN

'LENTEN is come with Love to town.' The theme of the anonymous lyric is the theme of almost the whole of Elizabethan poetry. Love was the power that moved the firmament; love was that which gave to men distinction and grace. From ladies' eyes came learning, and the lover's devotion to his mistress was an exercise in the refinement of the soul.

Yet this burden of the poets did not remain a melody of simple measures. While the lyrists sang of devotion and aspiration and despair, a darker note could be heard sounding on others' lips. Love, mysterious and to be desired, was also a disease, allied to the ominous melancholy adust—a passion apt to lead men not merely into temporary absurdity but even into complete corruption of the mind. Sometimes the very poets themselves who were most fervent in their exaltation of the virtues of love displayed an awareness of the danger confronting them.

And, in addition, there must be held in mind the universal belief that children owed to their parents an undeviating obedience. Perfect marriages, such as that of Ferdinand and Miranda, where the inclinations of the bridal pair coincided absolutely with parental wishes, were rare, and, even while worthy exponents of the current philosophy laid due stress upon the rights of fathers, many contemporaries harshly narrated the miseries of enforced marriage. The poets, of course, frequently escaped by directing their amorous effusions to ladies other than those they wished to wed or could have wedded, or else their verses were fashioned, not with one fair face in view, but with an idea of beauty in their minds; nevertheless, a discrepancy existed between a cult in which love was regarded as an all-powerful force and a current social philosophy which insisted that marriages should be profitable for parents. Children in a sense were assets. How conducive to the acquiring of riches they might be is demonstrated by the fact that many men, besides their own sons and daughters, sought to take under their care the children of others; the custody of a ward was then an advantageous occupation.

Love moveth all things. You that love shall move
All things in him, and he in you shall love.

For love is lord of truth and loyalty,
   Lifting himself out of the lowly dust.
On golden plumes up to the purest sky
   Above the reach of loathly sinful lust.

Love is a poison which spreadeth through 281
every vein; it is an herb that, being sown in the
entrails, mortifieth all the members; a pestilence
that through melancholy killeth the heart; and
the end of all virtues.

283   Let all dutiful and good-natured children, in the reverence and fear of God, consider what honour and obedience they do owe unto their parents and what power and authority He hath in his word sanctified unto them over their children in the Lord: in regard hereof, let them yield unto them this duty that, their fathers having provided for them such as are not of a wicked life, nor deformed or evil-favoured, nor of a contrary religion, they willingly submit themselves unto their choice.

284   There are two sorts in every perfect family: (1) the governors; (2) those that must be ruled.

285   The duties of a husband toward his wife are seven. (1) The first that he give honour to his wife as the weaker vessel, for she is partaker of the grace of life. (2) The second, he must patiently brook the hastiness of his wife, for there is nothing in the world more spiteful than a woman if she be hardly dealt withal, or egged to indignation. (3) The third duty, the husband in any case must not have carnal copulation with any other but his own wife. A woman is jealous and naturally suspicious, and, sith her husband breaketh with her, she will not stick to break with him and privily borrow a night's lodging with her neighbour. (4) The fourth duty, the husband must not injury his wife by word or deed, for a woman is a feeble creature and not endued with such a noble courage as the man; she is sooner pricked to the heart, or moved to passions, than man; and again, he that injurieth his wife, doth as if he should spit into the air and the same spittle return back upon his own self. (5) The fifth, the husband, in disputations with his wife, must sometimes confess himself vanquished by her. (6) The sixth, the husband must

provide for his wife and for her housekeeping according to his ability. (7) The seventh, the husband must suffer his wife to be merrily disposed before him, otherwise (a woman's nature is such) she will by stealth find out some secret place or other to tattle in and to disport herself.

But what shall the woman do? Shall she do what seemeth good in her own eyes? No: for St Peter speaketh unto wives in this wise: 'Let wives be subject to their husbands'—which is as much to say as they must not contradict them in any point, but rather endeavour to please them by all means. The second duty, the wife must not forsake her husband in adversity or deride him. The third, she must esteem the manners of her husband to be the legal rules of her life. The fourth, she must not be too sumptuous and superfluous in her attire, as decked with frizzled hair, embroidery, precious stones, gaudy raiments and gold put about, for they are the forerunners of adultery. The fifth, she must not be jealous or mistrust her husband's absence. The sixth duty of a wife is carefully to oversee her household, and to bring up her children and servants in the fear of God. The seventh, she must not discover her husband's imperfections and faults to any. The eighth duty of a wife is that she gibe not nor flout her husband, but bear with him as long as she may.

Although the women there are entirely in the power of their husbands except for their lives, yet they are not kept so strictly as they are in Spain or elsewhere. Nor are they shut up, but they have the free management of the house or housekeeping, after the fashion of those of the Netherlands and others their neighbours. They go to market to buy what they like best to eat. They are well-dressed, fond of taking it easy, and commonly leave the care of household matters and drudgery to their servants. They sit before their doors, decked out in fine clothes, in order to see and be seen by the passers-by. In all banquets and feasts they are shown the greatest honour; they are placed at the upper end of the table, where they are the first served; at the lower end they help the men. All the rest of their time they employ in walking and riding, in playing at cards

or otherwise, in visiting their friends and keeping company, conversing with their equals (whom they term 'gossips') and their neighbours, and making merry with them at childbirths, christenings, churchings and funerals; and all this with the permission and knowledge of their husbands, as such is the custom. Although the husbands often recommend to them the pains, industry and care of the German or Dutch women, who do what men ought to do both in the house and in the shops, for which services in England men are employed, nevertheless the women usually persist in retaining their customs. This is why England is called 'The Paradise of Married Women'.

A
Work worth the
Reading.

287

Wherein is contayned, fiue profitable and pithy Questions, very expedient, aswell for Parents to perceiue howe to bestowe their Children in marriage, and to dispose their goods at their death: as for all other Persons to receiue great profit by the rest of the matters herein expressed.

Newly published by *Charles Gibbon*.

The wisdome of a man commeth by using well his vacant time, and he that ceaseth from his owne matters and labour, may come by wisdome. Ecclef.38.24.

LONDON
Imprinted by *Thomas Orwin:* and are to be solde by *Henry Kyrkham*, dwelling at the little North doore of S. *Pauls Church*, at the signe of the *Blacke Boy*.
1591.

Parents ought to teach their children how to frame their gesture to a reverend and dutiful behaviour towards others, which consisteth in these points:

1. The first is to meet those that are coming towards them.

2. The second is to rise up to elders and betters when they pass by them.

3. The third duty of good manners to be observed in their gesture is to stand while their betters are sitting in place.

4. Their fourth duty is to bend the knee in token of humility and subjection.

5. The fifth thing is that they give the chief place to their betters.

6. Their last duty is to uncover their head.

Chastise thy child and imprint discipline in his heart while he is young and towardly, and thou shalt bow him to what instruction thou wilt.

EATING AND DRINKING

HABITS in eating and drinking were changing rapidly, but to the end of Elizabeth's reign some of the massive hospitality in simple foods which the age had inherited from former generations persisted in the great halls of country mansions. Perhaps the most characteristic feature of the Elizabethan table was its enormous variety—multitudes of dishes intended, not to be partaken course after course, but rather to be the subject of choice. The guests, often retaining their hats on their heads, sat long hours on their joint-stools while servitors brought to them the viands they preferred. Talk there was in plenty, but not clamour; more than one observer noted the 'gravity' and sober demeanour during meals.

In the preparing of the food, new and daintier methods were supplanting the old; herbs were freely used for giving flavour; and there was a passion for sweet-meats. The staple dishes were made of flesh, but it is important to note what a vast quantity of fish the Elizabethans consumed—or were forced to consume by royal command.

Naturally, views concerning drink sharply differed in accordance with the particular attitudes of observers; but there does not seem to be much doubt that excessive consumption of liquors increased towards the close of the century, largely because of the experiences of soldiers in the Low Countries. Even at the very beginning of the reign, however, a French visitor saw fit to comment on the Englishman's capacity for drink and on his habitual 'Good cheer' as he raised his tankard.

Imported wines were plentiful. Harrison declares there were fifty-six sorts of French wines known to him, as well as thirty Italian, Grecian and Spanish—

'whereof vernage, catepument, raspis, muscadel, romnie, bastard lire, osy caprie, clary and malmesey are not least of all accompted of because of their strength and valour'. In all of these the sweet-toothed Elizabethans loved to pour in quantities of sugar.

291 With us the nobility, gentry and students do ordinarily go to dinner at eleven before noon, and to supper at five, or between five and six at afternoon. The merchants dine and sup seldom before twelve at noon and six at night, especially in London. The husbandmen dine also at high noon, as they call it, and sup at seven or eight.

292 Concerning their diet, in number of dishes and change of meat the nobility of England do exceed most, having all things that either may be bought for money or gotten for the season. Gentlemen and merchants feed very finely, and a poor man it is that dineth with one dish.

293 We must have our tables furnished like poulters' stalls, or as though we were to victual Noah's Ark again (wherein there was all sorts of living creatures that ever were), or else the good-wife will not open her mouth to bid one welcome.

294 The English tables are not furnished with many dishes all for one man's diet, but severally for many men's appetite, and not only prepared for the family, but for strangers and relief of the poor. I confess that in such plenty and variety of meats every man cannot use moderation, nor understandeth that these several meats are not for one man but for several appetites, that each may take what he likes. And I confess that the English custom, first to serve gross meats, on which hunger spares not to feed, and then to serve dainties, which invite to eat without hunger, as likewise the long sitting and discoursing at tables, which makes men unawares eat more than the Italians can do at their solitary tables—these things, I say, give us just cause to cry with Socrates, 'God deliver me from meats that invite to eat beyond hunger.'

295 Here followeth the order of meats, how they must be served at the table, with their sauces for flesh days at dinner.

The first course

Potage or stewed broth, boiled meat or stewed meat, chickens and bacon, powdered beef, pies, goose, pig, roasted beef, roasted veal, custard.

The second course

Roasted lamb, roasted capons, roasted conies, chickens, peahens, baked venison, tart.

The first course at supper

A salad, a pig's pettitoe, powdered beef sliced, a shoulder of mutton or a breast, veal, lamb, custard.

The second course

Capons roasted, conies roasted, chickens roasted, pigeons roasted, larks roasted, a pie of pigeons or chickens, baked venison, tart.

The service at dinner

A dozen of quails, a dish of larks, two pasties of red deer in a dish, tart, gingerbread, fritters.

Of Roſe vvater out of Bulcaſis.

The makyuge of Roſewater is known in moſte coũtires. It is better made with water then without: better alſo by fire of cooles then of wood: wherfore of the iiii. waies whyche be withoute water wyth flaming woode: without water with coles: with water & flaming wood: with water and fire of cooles: the firſt is the worſt, and yeildeth a water of the leaſt ſmell: the ſecond is better then it: the third then the ſecond: but the fourth is beſt of all. The ſecond and the third are mooſte vſed. And I will here deſcribe thee third (whiche is made with water and woode flaming, as it is in vſe w̄ the kinges of Aharach. A. Thou ſhalt make therfore in a large houſe by a wall a litle berchile B ſo doth he cal the veſſel that is filled with water the bottom and ſides ſhalbe of leede, ſo wel cloſed, that it leek not in anye place. Then make meete a couering vnto this veſſel of glas or glaſed earth,

102

At this day the English inhabitants eat almost no flesh more commonly than hens, and for geese they eat them in two seasons, when they are fatted upon the stubble after harvest and when they are green about Whitsuntide, at which time they are held for dainties; and howsoever hares are thought to nourish melancholy, yet they are eaten as venison, both roasted and boiled. They have also great plenty of conies, the flesh whereof is fat, tender and much more delicate than any I have eaten in other parts.

Thus much of flesh. Now concerning fish which is no small part of our sustenance in this realm of England. And that flesh might be more plentiful and better cheap, two days in the week, that is Friday and Saturday, are specially appointed to fish, and now of late years by the providence of our prudent princess Elizabeth, the Wednesday also is in a manner restrained to the same order, not for any religion or holiness supposed to be in the eating of fish rather than of flesh, but only for a civil policy.

Forasmuch as our country is for the most part compassed with the seas and the greatest force for defence thereof, under God, is the Queen Majesty's navy of ships, for maintenance and increase of the said navy this law for abstinence hath been most carefully ordained, that, by the certain expense of fish, fishing and fishermen might be the more increased and the better maintained; for that the said trade is the chiefest nurse not only for the bringing up of youth for shipping, but great numbers of ships therein are used, furnished with sufficient mariners, men at all times in a readiness for Her Majesty's service in those affairs.

A Diet for Sanguine Men

Sanguine men be hot and moist of complexion, wherefore they must be circumspect in eating of their meat, considering that the purer the complexion is, the sooner it may be corrupted and the blood may be the sooner infected. Wherefore they must abstain to eat inordinately fruits and herbs, and roots as garlic, onions and leeks. They must refrain from eating of old flesh, and eschew the usage of eating of the brains of beasts and from eating the udders of kine.

A Diet for Phlegmatic Men

Phlegmatic men be cold and moist, wherefore they must abstain from meats the which is cold. And also they must refrain from eating viscous meat, specially from all meats the which doth ingender phlegmatic humours, as fish, fruit and white meat. These things be good for phlegmatic persons moderately taken—onions, garlic, pepper, ginger, and all meats the which be hot and dry.

A Diet for Choleric Men

Choler is hot and dry, wherefore choleric men must abstain from eating hot spices, and to refrain from drinking of wine and eating of choleric meat—howbeit choleric men may eat more grosser meat than any other of the complexions. The things following doth purge choler—fumitory, centory, wormwood, wild hops, violets, mercury, manna, rhubarb, eupatory, tamarindes and the whey of butter.

A Diet for Melancholy Men

Melancholy is cold and dry, wherefore melancholy men must refrain from fried meat and meat the which is over-salt, and from meat that is sour and hard of digestion, and from all meat the which is burned and dry. They must abstain from immoderate thirst and from drinking of hot wines and gross wine and red wine, and use these things—cow milk, almond milk, yolks of rere eggs. Boiled meat is better for melancholy men than roasted meats. These things following doth purge melancholy—quick beam, sene, sticados, hartstongue, maidenhair, puliol mountain, borage, organum, sugar and white wine.

To boil a capon with oranges and lemons

Take oranges and lemons peeled and cut them the long way, and if you can keep your cloves whole and put them into your best broth of mutton or capon with prunes or currants and three or four dates, and when these have been well sodden put whole pepper, great mace, a good piece of sugar, some rosewater and either white or claret wine, and let all these seethe together a while; and so serve it upon sops with your capon.

302

To make bake meats

Take a leg of lamb and cut out all the flesh, and save the skin whole; then mince it fine and white with it; then put in grated bread and some eggs, white and all, and some dates and currants; then season it with some pepper, cinammon, ginger and some nutmegs and carroways, and a little cream, and temper it all together; then put it into the leg of the lamb again and let it bake a little before you put it into your pie; and when you have put it into your pie, then put in a little of the pudding about it, and when it is almost baked, then put in verjuice, sugar and sweet butter, and so serve it.

To make a tart that is a courage to a man or woman

Take two quinces and two or three burre roots and a potato, and pare your potato, and scrape your roots and put them into a quart of wine, and let them boil till they be tender, and put in an ounce of dates and, when they be boiled tender, draw them through a strainer, wine and all; and then put in the yolks of eight eggs and the brains of three or four cock-sparrows, and strain them into the other, and a little rosewater, and seethe them all with sugar, cinammon and ginger and cloves and mace, and put in a little sweet butter, and set it upon a chafing-dish of coals between two platters, and so let it boil till it be something big.

From gluttony in meats let me descend to 303 superfluity in drink—a sin that ever since we have mixed ourselves with the Low Countries is counted honourable, but before we knew their lingering wars was held in the highest degree of hatred that might be.

Well fare, England, where the poor may have 304 a pot of ale for a penny—fresh ale, firm ale, nappy ale, nippitate ale, irregular, secular ale, courageous, contagious ale, alcumistical ale.

There is such heady ale and beer as for the 305 mightiness thereof among such as seek it out is commonly called 'huffcap', 'the mad dog', 'Father Whoreson', 'angels' food', 'dragon's milk', 'go-by-the-wall', 'stride wide' and 'lift leg', etc.

Clowns and vulgar men only use large drinking 306 of beer or ale. Gentlemen carouse only in wine, with which many mix sugar—which I never observed in any other place or kingdom to be used for that purpose. And because the taste of the English is thus delighted with sweetness, the wines in taverns (for I speak not of merchants' or gentlemen's cellars) are commonly mixed at the filling thereof, to make them pleasant.

Schools, Universities and
Foreign Travel

EDUCATION was a prime interest for an age conscious of its debt to classical learning, and children were forced, for their own good, to a severe regime. No doubt among the population as a whole there was a fair amount of illiteracy, but for the boys who lived within walking distance of any one of the many grammar schools ample opportunity was given for acquiring such a knowledge of Latin and Greek as might well be the envy of a university student today.

Of universities there were only two, but so many young gentlemen finished their academic training at the Inns of Court that contemporaries frequently referred to these as a third university, the university of London—and, moreover, in Gresham's academy was the beginning both of a research centre and of a popular home of learning, even more certainly pointing towards a metropolitan college.

Many students, we know, spent their time in frivolous reading and even more frivolous entertainment; but the 'scholar' was becoming a recognized type in the community, the kind of man who depended on intellectual accomplishments for his living—one who might become a playwright or a teacher or a clergyman in accordance with his predilections or fortune, and who, if he were not so successful as he deemed his attainments warranted, might, in self-pity, rend the air with bitter complaints and vicious castigation of contemporary society.

For the gentlemen, foreign travel constituted the finishing-school. True, numerous worthy souls regarded Italy, the Mecca of all wanderers, with abhorrence; true, too, those who dared to cross the Channel and the Alps hazarded many dangers and experienced many annoyances. No Englishman could leave the country without securing a passport, and his luggage was searched minutely at the coast to see whether he might not be taking with him more than the statutory ten pounds allowed to him; and, when he reached his destination, he frequently went in fear not merely of highway robbers but, more importantly, of Catholic agents anxious to seize upon his soul and his body. Fynes Moryson's experience was not unique: being in Rome at Lent, he learned that a priest had come to his house of lodging to take the names of all the dwellers therein, so that all might be present at the Easter Sacrament. 'Therefore', he says,

307 I went from Rome upon Tuesday before Easter and came to Siena upon Good Friday, and upon Easter even (pretending great business) took my journey to Florence, where I stayed only Easter day, and from thence went to Pisa, and before the end of Easter week returned in haste to Siena, where I had a chamber. Thus by often changing places I avoided the priests inquiring after me, which is most dangerous about Easter time, when all men receive the Sacrament.

But for the majority the joys of travel counterweighted the perils, and the possible evils were forgotten in the light of the positive good.

308

309 During the time of Her Majesty's most fortunate reign already, there hath been more schools erected than all the rest be that were before her time in the whole realm.

310 This course was in my time taken by the schoolmaster of Westminster for those of the sixth and seventh forms wherein I spent my time there.

About a quarter of an hour after five in the morning we were called up by one of the monitors of the chamber, with a 'Surgite!', and after Latin prayers we went into the cloisters to wash, and thence in order two by two to the school, where we were to be by six of the clock at the farthest. Between six and eight we repeated our grammar parts—out of Lilly for Latin, out of

106

Camden for the Greek—fourteen or fifteen being selected and called out to stand in a semicircle before the master and other scholars; and these repeated four or five leaves in either, the master appointing who should begin and who should go on with such and such rules. After this, we had two exercises that varied every other morning; the first morning we made verses extempore, Latin and Greek, upon two or three several themes, and they that made the best two or three of them had some money given them by the schoolmaster for the most part. The second morning one of the seventh form was called out to expound some part of a Latin or Greek author, Cicero, Livy, Isocrates, Homer, Apollinaris, Xenophon, etc. They of the two next forms were called to give an account of it some other part of the day, or else they were all of them (or such as were picked out of whom the master made choice by the fear or confidence discovered in their looks) to repeat and pronounce distinctly without book some piece of an author that had been learnt the day before.

From eight to nine we had beaver and recollection of ourselves and preparation for future exercises. Betwixt nine and eleven those exercises were made which had been enjoined us overnight (one day in prose, the next day in verse), which were selected by the master, some to be examined and punished, others to be commended and proposed to imitation—which being done, we had the practise of *dictamina*, one of the fifth form being called out to translate some sentence of an unexpected author, extempore, into good Latin, and then one of the sixth and seventh form to translate the same, extempore also, into good Greek. Then the master himself expounded some parts of a Latin or Greek author (one day in prose, another in verse) wherein we were to be practised that afternoon. At dinner and supper times we read some portion of the Latin in a manuscript (to facilitate the reading of such hands). And the prebendaries, then having their table commonly set in the hall, some of them had oftentimes good remembrances sent unto them from hence and withal a theme to make, or speak some extempore verses upon.

Betwixt one to three that lesson which, out of some author appointed for that day, had been by the master expounded unto them (out of Cicero, Virgil, Homer, Euripides, Isocrates, Livy, Sallust, etc.) was to be exactly gone through by construing and other grammatical ways, examining all the rhetorical figures and translating it out of verse into prose, or out of prose into verse, out of Greek into Latin or out of Latin into Greek. Then they were enjoined to commit that to memory against the next morning.

Betwixt three and four they had a little respite, the master walking out, and they (in beaver times) going in order to the hall and there fitting themselves for their next task.

Betwixt four and five they repeated a leaf or two out of some book of rhetorical figures or choice proverbs and sentences collected by the master for that use. After that they were practised in translating some *dictamina* out of Latin or Greek and sometimes turning Latin and Greek verse into English verse. Then a theme was given to them whereon to make prose and verse, Latin and Greek, against the next morning. After supper, in summer time, they were called to the master's chamber (specially those of the seventh form), and there instructed out of Hunter's *Cosmography*, and practised to describe and find out cities and countries in the maps.

I knew one who in winter would ordinarily, in 311 a cold morning, whip his boys over for no other purpose than to get himself a heat; another beat them for swearing, and all the while swears himself, with horrible oaths, he would forgive any fault saving that.

A YOUNG NOBLEMAN'S REGIMEN 312

First, to rise in such time as that he may be ready to his exercises by seven of the clock.
From seven until half hour after, dancing.
From that time until eight, breakfast.
From eight unto nine, French.
From thence to ten, Latin.
After ten one half hour in writing and dancing.
Then common prayers and so to dinner.

Afternoon's exercises

From one until two, cosmography.
From two until three, Latin.
From three until four, French.
From that time one half hour's exercise with his pen.
Then common prayers and so to supper.

On the holy days

To read before dinner the Epistle of the day in French, and after dinner the Gospel in Latin, or else to read both the Epistle and Gospel in the one tongue before dinner and in the other tongue after dinner, and to understand by some commentary any hard place: all the rest of the day to be spent in riding, shooting, dancing, walking and other commendable exercises, saving the times of prayer.

FATHER TO SON

I have received two letters from you, one written in Latin, the other in French; which I take in good part, and will you to exercise that practice of learning often: for that will stand you in most stead in that profession of life that you are born to live in. And, since this is my first letter that ever I did write to you, I will not that it be all empty of some advices which my natural care of you provoketh me to wish you to follow, as documents to you in this your tender age. Let your first action be the lifting up of your mind to Almighty God by hearty prayer, and feelingly digest the words you speak in prayer with continual meditation, and thinking of Him to whom you pray, and of the matter for which you pray. And use this as an ordinary, and at an ordinary hour—whereby the time itself will put you in remembrance to do that which you are accustomed to do. In that time apply your study, too, to such hours as your discreet master doth assign you, earnestly; and the time (I know) he will so limit as shall be both sufficient for your learning and safe for your health. And mark the sense and the matter of that you read, as well as the words. So shall you both enrich your tongue with words and your wit with matter; and judgment will grow as years groweth in you. Be

humble and obedient to your master, for unless you frame yourself to obey others—yea, and feel in yourself, what obedience is—you shall never be able to teach others how to obey you. Be courteous of gesture, and affable to all men, with diversity of reverence, according to the dignity of the person. There is nothing that winneth so much with so little cost. Use moderate diet, so as, after your meat, you may find your wit fresher and not duller, and your body more lively and not more heavy. Seldom drink wine, and yet sometime do, lest, being enforced to drink upon the sudden, you should find yourself inflamed. Use exercise of body, but such as is without peril of your joints or bones. It will increase your force, and enlarge your breath. Delight to be cleanly, as well in all parts of your body as in your garments. It shall make you grateful in each company, and otherwise loathsome. Give yourself to be merry, for you degenerate from your Father if you find not yourself most able in wit and body to do any thing when you be most merry: but let your mirth be ever void of all scurrility and biting words to any man, for a wound given by a word is oftentimes harder to be cured than that which is given with the sword. Be you rather a hearer, and bearer away of other men's talk than a beginner or procurer of speech, otherwise you shall be counted to delight to hear yourself speak. If you hear a wise sentence or an apt phrase, commit it to your memory, with respect of the circumstance when you shall speak it. Let never oath be heard to come out of your mouth, nor word of ribaldry; detest it in others, so shall custom make to yourself a law against it in yourself. Be modest in each assembly, and rather be rebuked of light fellows for maidenlike shamefastness than of your sad friends for pert boldness. Think upon every word that you will speak before you utter it, and remember how nature hath rampired up (as it were) the tongue with teeth, lips, yea, and hair without the lips, and all betokening reins, or bridles, for the loose use of that member. Above all things tell no untruth, no, not in trifles. The custom of it is naught, and let it not satisfy you that, for a time, the hearers take it for a truth; for after it will be known as it is to your shame; for there cannot be

315

a greater reproach to a gentleman than to be accounted a liar. Study and endeavour yourself to be virtuously occupied. So shall you make such an habit of well doing in you that you shall not know how to do evil, though you would. Remember, my son, the noble blood you are descended of, by your Mother's side; and think that only by virtuous life and good action you may be an ornament to that illustrious family; and otherwise, through vice and sloth, you shall be counted *labes generis*, one of the greatest curses that can happen to man. Well (my little Philip) this is enough for me, and too much I fear for you. But, if I shall find that this light meal of digestion nourish anything the weak stomach of your young capacity, I will, as I find the same grow stronger, feed it with tougher food.

Your loving Father, so long as you live

in the fear of God,

H. SYDNEY

316   In my time there are three noble universities in England—to wit, one at Oxford, the second at Cambridge, and the third in London: of which the first two are the most famous for that in them the use of the tongues, philosophy and the liberal sciences, besides the profound studies of the civil law, physic and theology, are daily taught and had, whereas in the latter the laws of the realm are only read and learned by such as give their minds unto the knowledge of the same.

317   The first degree is that of the general sophisters, from whence, when they have learned more sufficiently the rules of logic, rhetoric, and obtained thereto competent skill in philosophy and in the mathematicals, they ascend higher unto the estate of bachelors of art, after four years of their entrance into their sophistry. From thence also, giving their minds to more perfect knowledge in some or all the other liberal sciences and the tongues, they rise at the last (to wit, after other three or four years) to be called masters of art. After this they are permitted to choose what other of the higher studies them liketh to follow, whether it be divinity, law or physic, so that,

being once masters of art, the next degree, if they follow physic, is the doctorship belonging to that profession, and likewise in the study of the law, if they bend their minds to the knowledge of the same.

Thus we see that from our entrance into the university unto the last degree received is commonly eighteen or peradventure twenty years.

318   Last of all, Sir Thomas Gresham, knight, agent to the Queen's Highness, by his last will and testament made in the year 1579 gave the Royal Exchange and all the buildings thereunto appertaining, that is to say, the one moity to the Mayor and Communality of London and their successors upon trust that they perform as shall be declared; and the other moity to the Mercers in like confidence. The Mayor and Communality are to find four to read lectures of Divinity, Astronomy, Music and Geometry within his dwellinghouse in Bishopsgate-street, and to bestow the sum of £200, to wit, £50 the piece etc. The Mercers likewise are to find three Readers, that is in Civil Law, Physic and Rhetoric, within the same dwellinghouse, the sum of £150, to every Reader £50 etc. The lecturers were accordingly chosen and appointed to have begun their readings in the month of June 1597. These lectures are read daily, Sundays excepted, in the term times by every one upon his day, in the morning betwixt nine and ten, in Latin; in the afternoon, betwixt two and three, in English.

319   One came into a college in an university and asked how many Fellows belonged to the house. Another replied that there were more good fellows than good scholars, two to one.

320   Go to the learned universities
    And tell the scholars of the loss of time.
Bid them beware of too much liberties—
    Best-thriving plants are tended in their prime;
And bid them first go read the rules of grace,
That lower blessings may come on apace.

321   Who's yonder
Deep-mouth'd hound that bellows rimes like
    thunder?
He makes an earthquake throughout Paul's
    churchyard—
Well fare his heart, his 'larum shall be heard.
O he's a puisne of the Inns of Court
Come from th' university to make sport
With his friends' money here.

322   Though gentility be of itself gracious, yet it
is much more excellent when it is adorned with
the experience of foreign countries.

323 Base and vulgar spirits hover still about
home; those are more noble and divine that
imitate the heavens and joy in motion.

324 Yet I must confess much dross with this gold
and to many ills be they subject which travel in
foreign countries, the body by dissoluteness
overthrown, the soul spotted and corrupted with
a multitude of villainies as atheism, self love,
dissimulation and fantastical giddities.

325 Suffer not thy sons to pass the Alps, for they
shall learn nothing there but pride, blasphemy
and atheism.

Science and Physic

THIS was not an age of science. Certainly there were men who, in divers realms, were pressing forward towards the goal of Bacon's dreams, and several important discoveries were being made, of which chief perhaps is William Gilbert's study of magnetism in 1600. To the succeeding generations, however, were to be left the first sure advancements in scientific thought. The results of Harvey's epoch-making investigation of the blood circulation were not announced until 1616 and were not published until 1628. A Royal Society for the advancement of science did not come until an entirely new age dawned under Charles II.

Dimly, but only dimly, Elizabeth's England glimpsed the vision of a medical faculty, trained in the art of healing and powerful enough to prevent the malpractices of charlatans. So long as men thought it part of their education to become ministers of the sick at home, so long as wise women and wizards laid a spell on the popular mind, there was little possibility of a rational development of medical knowledge. And so long as both the unlettered ploughman and the learned scholar put faith in the hidden properties of things, exact scientific method was an impossibility.

We need not, however, in the superiority of our post-Cartesian wisdom look down with scorn on the sixteenth-century's scientific shortcomings. The wisdom of that age was a deep wisdom, and, if it was set on a basis different from ours, it need not therefore be despised. A Shakespeare was possible then; a Shakespeare since has not been found.

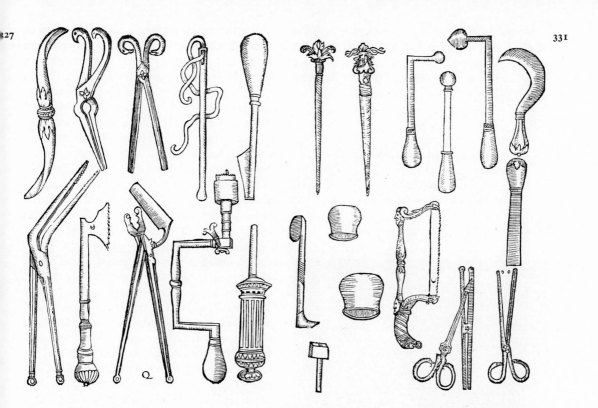

328 The scope of physic is to glorify God in the works of nature, teaching men to live well and to help their neighbours.

29   A worthy physician is the enemy of sickness, in purging nature from corruption. His action is most in feeling of pulses, and his discourses chiefly of the nature of diseases. He is a great searcher-out of simples, and accordingly makes his composition. He persuades abstinence and patience for the benefit of health, while purging and bleeding are the chief courses of his counsel.

A MERE DULL PHYSICIAN

30 His practice is some business at bedsides, and his speculation an urinal. The best cure he has done is upon his own purse, which from a lean sickliness he hath made lusty and in flesh. His learning consists much in reckoning up the hard names of diseases and the superscriptions of gallipots in his apothecary's shop, which are ranked in his shelves and the doctor's memory. Of all odours he likes best the smell of urine, and holds Vespatian's rule, that no gain is unsavoury. If you send this once to him, you must resolve to be sick howsoever, for he will never leave examining your water till he have shaked it into a disease. Then follows a writ to his drugger in a strange tongue, which he understands though he cannot conster. He tells you your malady in Greek, though it be but a cold or headache—which by good endeavour and diligence he may bring to some moment indeed. If he have leisure to be idle—that is, to study—he has a smatch at alchemy, and is sick of the philosopher's stone, a disease uncurable but by an abundant phlebotomy of the purse.

332 How is the same physician called?
'He is called Doctor N. of London.'
Is he learned and an honest man, tell me?
'He is sufficient to kill one or two.'

333   Nowadays every man, tag and rag, of what insufficiency soever, is suffered to exercise the mystery of physic and surgery, and to minister both the one and the other to the diseased and infirm persons—but to their woe, you may be sure.

334
As for our physicians,
  their cunning knoweth how
As well to kill as to purloin:
  they are expert in all.
One hath a potion for to serve
  and cure each kind of grief;
He'll sell a quart for forty pence.

335

336   In this my collection, gentle and virtuous reader, I mean by God's permission and your courteous patience here truly and faithfully to deliver unto thy view the manifold and injurious abuses of a disordered number of prowling women, daily practising physic and chirurgery within this city of London and the liberties of the same, whose knowledge and judgments, I say, is fallible and uncertain, whereby they are the causes of many hidden mischiefs. There is, I say, known to be in London which daily do practise chirurgery of strange women born beyond the seas, called of some cunning or wise women, more in number than there are of surgeons lawfully allowed and admitted, according unto the laws and statutes of this realm, being fit men to do Her Majesty service in their art. There be also in like manner at this present to be found in London, besides those aforesaid, of our own countrywomen that hath neither wit nor art, which daily practise physic and chirurgery, far more in number than there is of the strange women. It may seem uncredible that there is not at this present time of sufficient and able chirurgeons to be found in London scarce half the number which were lately employed in Her Majesty's service with General Norris and Sir Francis Drake. And yet the greater sort of those that are gone are very poor men, and so poor indeed that some of them went out very slenderly furnished—some with a little chirurgery stuff in a scholar's satchel, other some in budgets and bags, being very unfit furniture to serve in Her Majesty's service. Unfortunate and unhappy shall that soldier be that tasteth of these surgeons' wants.

337
My kitchen is my doctor; and my garden
My college, master, chief assistant, warden
And 'potecary.

¶ The newe Iewell of Health, wherein is

contayned the moſt excellent Secretes of Phiſicke and Philoſophie, deuided into fower Bookes. In the which are the beſt approued remedies for the diſeaſes as well inwarde as outwarde, of all the partes of mans bodie : treating very amplye of all Dyſtillations of Waters, of Oyles, Balmes, Quinteſſences, with the extraction of artificiall Saltes, the vſe and preparation of Antimonie, and potable Gold. Gathered out of the beſt and moſt approued Authors, by that excellent Doctor *Geſnerus.* Alſo the Pictures, and maner to make the Veſſels, Furnaces, and other Inſtrumentes therevnto belonging. Faithfully corrected and publiſhed in Engliſhe,
by George Baker, Chirurgian.

ALCHYMYA.

338

Printed at London, by Henrie Denham.
1576.

For physic some again he inwardly applies.
For comforting the spleen and liver gets for juice
Pale hore-hound, which he holds of most especial
    use.
So saxifrage is good, and hart's-tongue for the
    stone,
With agrimony and that herb we call St John.
To him that hath a flux of shepherd's-purse he
    gives,
And mouse-ear unto him whom some sharp
    rupture grieves.
And for the labouring wretch that's troubled
    with a cough
Or stopping of the breath by phlegm that's hard
    and tough
Campana here he crops, approvèd wondrous
    good—
As comfrey unto him that's bruisèd, spitting
    blood;
And from the falling-ill by five-leaf doth restore,
And melancholy cures by sovereign hellebore.

340 Here finds he on an oak rheum-purging polipode,
And in some open place that to the sun doth lie
He fumitory gets, and eye-bright for the eye;
The yarrow, wherewithal he stops the wound-
    made gore;
The healing tutsan then, and plantan for a sore.
And hard by them again he holy vervain finds,
Which he about his head that hath the megrim
    binds.
The wonder-working dill he gets not far from
    these,
Which curious women use in many a nice disease.
For them that are with newts, or snakes, or
    adders stung
He seeketh out an herb that's callèd adder's
    tongue,
As Nature it ordain'd its own like hurt to cure
And sportive did herself to niceties inure.
Valerian then he crops, and purposely doth
    stamp
T'apply unto the place that's halèd with the
    cramp.
As centory, to close the wideness of a wound,
The belly hurt by birth by mugwort to make
    sound.
His chickweed cures the heat that in the face
    doth rise.

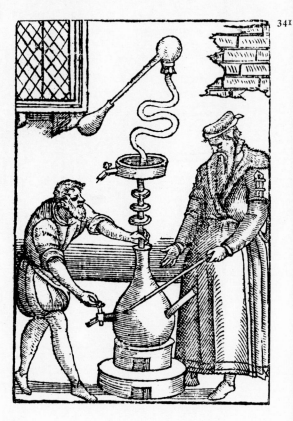

341

There are virtues in things, which belong not to any element. They are called hidden properties, because their causes are hidden so that man's understanding is not able in any wise to find them out. Wherefore the philosophers have attained to a very great part of them by long experience more than by the search of reason.

All men know that the loadstone hath a certain virtue wherewith he draweth iron and that the diamond with his presence taketh away the virtue of the loadstone. Amber and jet, being rubbed and warmed, draweth chaff or straw. The stone *abeston*, being kindled, is never or scarcely quenched. The carbuncle giveth light in darkness. *Aetites*, or the eagle's stone, being laid upon, doth strengthen the offspring of women and plants, and, laid underneath, draweth them. The jasper stone stauncheth blood; the little fish *eckines* stayeth a ship; rhubarb expelleth choler; the liver of the chameleon, burned upon the tiles of a house, raiseth rain and thunder. The stone *heliotropius* doth dazzle the eyes and maketh him that carrieth it invisible. The stone *lincurius*

taketh away illusions from the eyes. The fumigation of *lipparis* maketh all beasts to come abroad. *Synochitides* bringeth out the ghosts below.

The Arts

MUSIC AND THE DANCE

THIS was an age of music and dance—not the music of great composers or the professional ballet, but the native song, the familiar playing of instruments, the continual breaking out into country rounds or court measures. If England, because of the stern frowns of the Puritans, had no opportunity of hearing and of creating great church music, her people found widespread joy in madrigals, glees and catches. Every house had its lutes and viols, every barber's shop had an instrument ready for the hands of its waiting customers. In the theatre, song was an integral part of plays, and music before and during the performance formed part of the attraction of the 'private' houses. Ballads were sung in the streets and at the innumerable fairs.

Characteristic of the period was the 'chest of viols' and the pleasantly rounded lute, with its somewhat rarer and larger cousin, the arch-lute or theorbo. Recorders and hautboys were perhaps more professional instruments, but great ladies, the Queen herself, delighted in the delicate sounds of the virginals, the ancestor of the modern piano. Shakespeare's knowledge, use and love of music was but typical.

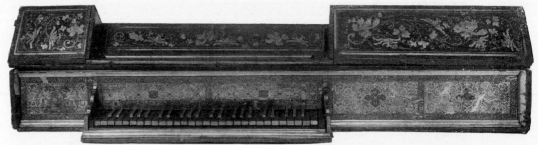

345

346   Take Arts away,
Men are but painted loam and gilded clay.

347   As the heart ruleth over all the members, so
music overcometh the heart.

348   My Lord of Hunsdon drew me up to a quiet
gallery where I might hear the Queen play upon
the virginals. After I had hearkened awhile,
I took by the tapestry that hung before the door
of the chamber and, seeing her back was toward
the door, I entered within the chamber, and
stood a pretty space hearing her play excellently
well; but she left off immediately so soon as she
turned her about and saw me. She appeared to
be surprised to see me and came forward, seeming
to strike me with her hand, alleging she used not
to play before men, but when she was solitary, to
shun melancholy.

349 If music and sweet poetry agree,
        As they must needs (the sister and the brother),
    Then must the love be great twixt thee and me,
        Because thou lov'st the one and I the other.
    Dowland to thee is dear, whose heavenly touch
        Upon the lute doth ravish human sense;
    Spenser to me, whose deep conceit is such
        As, passing all conceit, needs no defence.
    Thou lov'st to hear the sweet melodious sound
        That Phoebus' lute, the queen of music,
            makes,
    And I in deep delight am chiefly drown'd
        When as himself to singing he betakes.

That harmony which is skilfully expressed by   350
instruments, albeit by reason of the variety of
number and proportion of itself it easily stirs up
the minds of the hearers to admiration and
delight, yet far higher authority and power hath
been ever worthily attributed to that kind of
music which to the sweetness of instrument
applies the lively voice of man, expressing some
worthy sentence or excellent poem. So that Plato
defines melody to consist of harmony, number
and words—harmony, naked of itself; words, the
ornament of harmony; number, the common
friend and uniter of them both.

Do you sing it, and I'll dance it.   351

If you speak of the kind of dancing that is   352
received with us in every place where dancing is
used, all good consciences must needs condemn
it. For is it a seemly thing, think you, that a

353

122

Christian man or a Christian woman should be so much delighted with hearing a profane, and sometimes a filthy, song played upon an instrument that they should leap for joy at the hearing of it?

    As men more civil grew,
 Love did more grave and solemn measures
    frame,
With such fair order and proportion true
 And correspondence every way the same
That no fault-finding eye did ever blame,
 For every eye was movèd at the sight
With sober wond'ring and with sweet delight.

Not those old students of the heavenly book,
 Atlas the great, Prometheus the wise,
Which on the stars did all their life-time look,
 Could ever find such measures in the skies,
 So full of change and rare varieties;
Yet all the feet whereon these measures go
Are only spondees, solemn, grave and slow.

THE GALLIARD   356

But for more diverse and more pleasing show
 A swift and wandering dance she did invent—
With passages uncertain, to and fro,
 Yet with a certain answer and consent
 To the quick music of the instrument.
Five was the number of the music's feet,
Which still the dance did with five paces meet.

A gallant dance! that lively doth bewray
 A spirit and a virtue masculine,
Impatient that her house on earth should stay,
 Since she herself is fiery and divine.
 Oft doth she make her body upward flyne
With lofty turns and caprioles in the air,
Which with the lusty tunes accordeth fair.

THE CORANTO   357

What shall I name those current travases
 That on a triple dactyl foot do run
Close by the ground, with sliding passages,
 Wherein that dancer greatest praise hath won

Which with best order can all orders shun?
For everywhere he wantonly must range,
And turn and wind with unexpected change.

358   THE LAVOLTA

Yet is there one, the most delightful kind,
  A lofty jumping, or a leaping round,
When arm in arm two dancers are entwined
    And whirl themselves, with strict embrace-
      ments bound,
    And still their feet an anapœst do sound—
An anapæst is all their music's song,
Whose first two feet are short, and third is long.

359   THE PAVAN

Then a dance was begun. Men and women
linked hands as in Germany. The men donned
their hats or bonnets, although otherwise no one,
however exalted his rank, may put on his hat in
the Queen's chamber, whether she be present or
not. The dancers danced behind one another as
in Germany, and all the dancers, ladies and
gentlemen, wore gloves. Though the dance at
first sight seemed to be of German nature, it was
no German dance, for they made a few steps
forward and then back again. Finally they
separated. The couples changed among one
another, but at the right moment each dancer
returned to his or her partner. While dancing
they very often courtesied to one another and
every time the men bowed before their lady
partners they doffed their hats. This dance was
danced only by the most eminent who were no
longer very young.

36

        Dancing began to be   36
When the first seeds whereof the world did
  spring,
The Fire, Air, Earth and Water, did agree
  By Love's persuasion, Nature's mighty King,
  To leave their first disordered combating
And in a dance such measure to observe
As all the world their motion should preserve.

Since when, they still are carried in a round
  And, changing, come one in another's place;
Yet do they neither mingle nor confound,
  But every one doth keep the bounded space
  Wherein the dance doth bid it turn or trace.
This wondrous miracle did Love devise,
For dancing is Love's proper exercise.

LITERATURE

OBVIOUSLY, it is by its contributions to prose and poetry that the Elizabethan
age is now most securely remembered. Men of this time did not merely acquire
a supreme power of self-expression, they also had the power to express the
spirit of their time. In the Romantic period the most characteristic writers

might retire to solitude with Wordsworth or seek escape abroad with Shelley; during the Elizabethan age almost every poet was set directly in the centre of life.

Like a heady wine, the language of the time intoxicated the young men attracted to literature. Every week, every day, every hour new words were being coined, new phrases minted; the power of words was recognized as possessing almost magical strength, and rhetoric, the art of persuasion, was eagerly studied that its secrets might be revealed and put to new uses.

In some circles the older 'genteel' tradition endured, whereby it was not thought fitting for men of noble birth to publish the things they wrote, but the printing-press, for good or ill, had now come to be a potent force and literature, prevailingly reserved in the past for a privileged few, had become a possession of the people. Although sugared sonnets and other literary compositions could still be handed round in manuscript for private reading, the characteristic writings were those which appeared from one among the dozens of presses in cheap quarto or more ambitious folio form and which anyone could consult and purchase at the booksellers' booths in Paul's Churchyard.

362 Power above powers, O heavenly Eloquence,
　　That with the strong rein of commanding
　　　　words
Dost manage, guide and master th' eminence
　　Of men's affections more than all their swords:
Shall we not offer to thy excellence
　　The richest treasure that our wit affords?

Thou that canst do much more with one poor pen
　　Than all the powers of princes can effect,
And draw, divert, dispose and fashion men
　　Better than force or rigour can direct—
Should we this ornament of glory then
　　As th' unmaterial fruits of shades neglect?

Or should we careless come behind the rest
　　In power of words, that go before in worth,
Whenas our accents equal to the best
　　Is able greater wonders to bring forth,
When all that ever hotter spirits expressed
　　Comes bettered by the patience of the North?

And who in time knows whither we may vent
　　The treasure of our tongue, to what strange
　　　　shores
This gain of our best glory shall be sent
　　T' enrich unknowing nations with our stores?

What worlds in th' yet unformèd Occident
　　May come refin'd with th' accents that are
　　　　ours?

It is the new fashion speech that troubleth me. 363 'I beseech you, sir, shew the abuse thereof, for I am persuaded the singularity or marvellous fineness therein troubleth the whole world.' I am contented to shew you their crippledness that I have observed to halt in that kind. Some speak as if they had a mint going in their mouths and lack a stamp to figure their words. Others speak as though they were matching their words as fletchers do arrow heads to their shafts. Others speak as though their words were hidebound in their mouths and lack a mash of liquorice and raisins of the sun to loose their tongues. Others keep their mouths shut up a long while, to make their words strong and forcible, on purpose to shoot birdbolts. Others have such a sharp loose in letting go of their words that they are able to make you an answer before they know your demand. Others speak so scornfully as though they bought their words by wholesale and were too good to retail them again. Other some speak

125

364

their words so thick that you must tarry the chewing them ere you can conceive what they say. Others speak with such a grace of moral sentences and phrases that you would think that they eat no other meat but apothegms and dictionaries. Others keep a school of manners in their mouth, every word giving back, to have the other go before. Others speak such spangled words that you would think they had them all at the embroiderers: such commonly never spare for any cost. Others speak such odoriferous, provocative words that you would imagine them to be made of ambergrice: when such open their mouths all the coast is perfumed as it was when Cleopatra breathed upon wanton Antony.

'Had I not crossed myself and removed out of your circle, I had been a dead man ere this.'

Why, man, shew me the bug that we may run away both together.

'Your word "odoriferous" hath made every joint of me to tremble and shake, and my hair to stare and stand upright on my head, as you see.'

365

Books are companions and friends and counsel- 366
lors, and therefore ought to be civil, honest and discreet, lest they corrupt with false doctrine, rude manners and vicious living.

No manner of person shall print any manner of 367
book or paper of what sort, nature, or in what language soever it be, except the same be first licensed by Her Majesty by express words in writing, or by six of her Privy Council, or be perused and licensed by the Archbishops of Canterbury and York, the Bishop of London, the Chancellors of both Universities.

PUBLISHER AND POET 368

Poet. Danter, thou art deceived: wit is dearer than thou takest it to be. I tell thee this libel of Cambridge has much salt and pepper in the nose. It will sell sheerly underhand whenas these books of exhortations and catechisms lie moulding on thy shopboard.

Publisher. It's true; but, good faith, Mr Ingenioso, I lost by your last book, and you know there is many a one that pays me largely for the printing of their inventions. But for all this, you shall have forty shillings and an odd pottle of wine.

Poet. Forty shillings! A fit reward for one of your rheumatic poets, that beslavers all the paper he comes by, and furnishes the chandlers with waste papers to wrap candles in! But as for me, I'll be paid dear even for the dregs of my wit. Little knows the world what belongs to the keeping of a good wit in waters, diets, drinks, tobacco, etc. It is a dainty and costly creature, and therefore I must be paid sweetly. Furnish me with money, that I may put myself in a new suit of clothes, and I'll suit thy shop with a new suit of terms: it's the gallantest child my invention was ever delivered of. The title is: *A Chronicle of Cambridge Cuckolds.* Here a man may see what day of the month such a man's commons were enclosed and when thrown open, and when any entailed some odd crowns upon the heirs of their bodies unlawfully begotten. Speak quickly, else I am gone.

Publisher. O this will sell gallantly! I'll have it whatsoever it cost. Will you walk on, Mr Ingenioso? We'll sit over a cup of wine and agree on it.

POET AND PATRON

Patron. How now, fellow, have you anything to say to me?

Poet. Pardon, sir, the presumption of a poor scholar, whose humble, devoted ears being familiar with the commendations that unpartial fame bestoweth upon your worship, reporting what a free-hearted Maecenas you are unto poor artists, that other favourers of learning in comparison of your worship are unworthy to untie your worship's purse-strings, that it hath been your ancient desire to get witty subjects for your liberality, that you could never endure the seven liberal sciences to carry their fardles on their backs like footmen but have animated their poor dying pens and put life to their decayed purses—hereupon I, unfurnished of all things but learning, cast myself down at your worship's toes, resolving that liberality sojourneth here with you, or else it hath clean left our untoward country. Take in good part, I beseech you, your own eternity, my pains, wherein in the ages to come men shall read your praises and give a shrewd guess at your virtues.

Patron (*he reads in the epistle dedicatory this sentence*). 'Desolate eloquence and forlorn poetry, your most humble suppliants *in forma pauperum*, lay prostrate at your dainty feet and adore your excellency, etc.' (*He nods his head.*) I do in some sort like this sentence, for in my days I have been a great favourer of scholars; but surely of late the *utensilia* of potions and purges have been very costly unto me. For my own part, I had not cared for dying, but when I am dead I know not what will become of scholars: hitherto I have besprinkled them prettily with the drops of my bounty.

Poet. O, your worship may be bold with yourself! No other tongue will be so niggard as to call

Soon mayest thou grovel in the lowly dust
And ne'er be spoken of but in obloquy.
And if I live, I'll make a poesie
Shall load thy future years with infamy.

I acknowledge an entire debt not only of my 372
best knowledge, but of all, yea, of more than
I know or can, to your bounteous lordship, most
noble, most virtuous and most honorable Earl of
Southampton, in whose pay and patronage I have
lived some years, to whom I owe and vow the
years I have to live.

Among the innumerable sorts of English books 373
and infinite fardles of printed pamphlets wherewith this country is pestered, all shops stuffed
and every study furnished, the greatest part,
I think, in any one kind are such as are either
mere poetical or which tend in some respect (as
either in matter or form) to poetry.

Ye modern laureates, famoused for your writ, 374
   Who for your pregnance may in Delos dwell,
On your sweet lines Eternity doth sit,
   Their brows ennobling with applause and
     laurel.

those drops, which indeed are plenteous showers,
that so often have refreshed thirsty brains and
sunburnt wits. And might it now please the
cloud of your bounty to break, it never found a
drier soil to work upon, or a ground that will
yield a more plenteous requital.

Patron. Indeed, these lines are pretty, and in
time thou mayest do well. I have not leisure as
yet to read over this book, yet, howsoever, I do
accept of thy duty and will do something if
occasion serve. In the meantime, hold, take a
reward. (*He gives him two groats.*) I tell thee,
Homer had scarce so much bestowed upon him
in all his lifetime: indeed, our countenance is
enough for a scholar, and the sunshine of our
favour yields good heat of itself. Howsoever,
I am somewhat prodigal that way, in joining gifts
to my countenance: yet it is fit that all such young
men as you are should know that all duty is far
inferior to our deserts that in great humility do
vouchsafe to read your labours. (*Exit.*)

Poet. Go, in a pox, and ne'er return again,
Thou lave-ear'd ass that loves dross more than
    arts!
Farewell, gross piece of earth, base bragging
    dung;

375

9   **129**   N C

378   *Marlowe*, bathèd in the Thespian springs,
Had in him those brave translunary things
That the first poets had. His raptures were
All air and fire, which made his verses clear;
For that fine madness still he did retain
Which rightly should possess a poet's brain.

   And surely *Nashe*, though he a proser were,
A branch of laurel yet deserves to bear;
Sharply satiric was he, and that way
He went, since that his being to this day,
Few have attempted—and I surely think
Those words shall hardly be set down with ink
Shall scorch and blast so as his could, where he
Would inflict vengeance. And be it said of thee,
Shakespeare, thou hadst as smooth a comic vein
Fitting the sock, and in thy natural brain
As strong conception and as clear a rage,
As any one that traffic'd with the stage.

Amongst these *Samuel Daniel*, whom if I
May speak of, but to censure do deny,
Only have heard some wise men him rehearse
To be too much historian in verse;
His rimes were smooth, his metres well did close,
But yet his manner better fitted prose.
Next these learn'd *Jonson* in this list I bring,
Who had drunk deep of the Pierian spring,
Whose knowledge did him worthily prefer,
And long was lord here of the theatre.

The means whereby men from time to time 380
have been preferred even to the highest degrees
of greatness and dignity have ever been and are
of two sorts—arms and letters, weapons and
books.

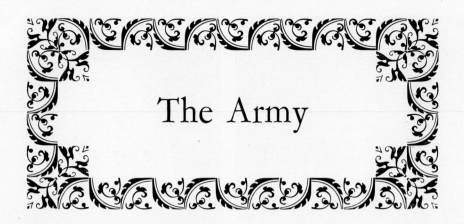

The Army

IN 1596 the Venetian agent, Francesco Gradenigo, sent to the Doge a letter descriptive of his experiences in England. 'Against all invasion in force', he wrote, 'they have this, to me, admirable arrangement. The whole country is diversified by charming hills, and from the summits of those which are nearer to the sea they sweep the whole horizon. On these summits are poles with braziers filled with inflammable material which is fired by the sentinel if armed ships of the enemy are sighted, and so in a moment the news spreads from hill to hill throughout the kingdom.'

This letter, written eight years after the Armada had been shattered, well illustrates the constant menace of invasion which confronted England during the whole of Elizabeth's reign. Such menace, however, proved exhilarating rather than oppressive. It is true that war's horrors weighed on many minds; but here two opposing concepts clashed. On the one hand, Elizabeth was praised for the long period of peace which she precariously sustained during her earlier years; on the other, the fear of what peace brings with it, associated with the natural valiancy of the age, made battle's alarms sound pleasantly stirring.

No doubt many of those who were mustered into military service made unwilling soldiers, yet the troops who fought in the Low Countries and elsewhere were by no means made up of youths pressed by force into disordered battalions—the number of volunteers who trailed their pikes abroad testifies to that. Ben Jonson was of their company, and Shakespeare may have been.

What Elizabethans feared was civil war, for the long and disastrous Wars of the Roses remained a potent terror in the memory. War with other lands, particularly when it involved fighting for a faith and an established way of life, evoked no such fears; the trained bands turned out with a will and the Queen's famous speech to her forces at Tilbury exactly caught the mood of the time.

382 The drums and clarions sound, and now behold
    Our Soldier, rampant-like, nor umbreant-like,
Bloodily tearing princes' throats for gold,
    Or playing the mole. His sword does fairly
        strike.
    He talks with cannons' mouths, and by his
        pike
Measures out peace (peace is woven out of war).
He's paralleled with kings: kings, soldiers are.

Upon his head grow bays (proof against lightning
    And thundering terrors); on his heart a rock
Which gives to his own nation strength and
    heightening,
    To others shipwrack. He's the waking cock,
    The Delphic oracle to which we flock
When hard things happen. He's (when dangers
    call)
The court's guard, country's bulwark, city's
    wall.

383

As for able men for service, thanked be God! 384 we are not without good store; for, by the musters taken 1574 and 1575, our number amounted to 1,172,674, and yet were they not so narrowly taken but that a third part of this like multitude was left unbilled and uncalled.

In England, when service happeneth, we dis- 385 burthen the prisons of thieves, we rob the taverns and alehouses of tosspots and ruffians, we scour both town and country of rogues and vagabonds.

THE ORDERS WHICH ARE TO BE OBSERVED 386
FOR THE FURNISHING OF WEAPONS

Calivers or Harquebuziers or Musketeers

Such must have either of them a good and sufficient piece, flash, touch-bore, powder, shot, iron, mould, worm, tireball, rammer, sword and dagger, and a morion.

Archers or Long-bows

Necessary is it that every man have a good and meet bow according to his draught and strength, light and easy, a light side-jack hanging loose to his knee, with a skull, sword and dagger, nothing upon his arms, whereby in time of service he may easily draw the arrow to the head, that they may deliver the same with strength and art, as Englishmen be accustomed.

Pikemen

Those bearing that warlike weapon, especially the fronts, where sometimes captains, lieutenants,

387

Our armour differeth not from that of other nations, and therefore consisteth of corslets, almaine rivets, shirts of mail, jacks quilted and covered over with leather, fustian or canvas, over thick plates of iron that are sewed in the same, and of which there is no town or village that hath not her convenient furniture. The said armour and munition likewise is kept in one several place of every town, appointed by the consent of the whole parish, where it is always ready to be had and worn within an hour's warning. Certes there is almost no village so poor in England (be it never so small) that hath not sufficient furniture in a readiness to set forth three or four soldiers, as one archer, one gunner, one pike and a billman at the least. As for the armories of some of the nobility, they are so well furnished that within some one baron's custody I have seen three score or a hundred corslets at once, beside calivers, hand-guns, bows, sheaves of arrows, pikes, bills, poleaxes, flasks, touchboxes, targets, etc., the very sight whereof appalled my courage.

388

sergeants and cavaliers of bands be oftentimes planted with pikes, and is the place for gentlemen to serve in, must have a fair Milan corslet, with all pieces appertaining to the same—that is, the curats, the collars, the pouldrons, with the vambraces, also the long tasses with the burgonet, with sword and dagger, their pikes of the usual length.

Halberdiers or Billmen

These be guards unto captains and ensigns, which be most times chosen gentlemen of experience or cavaliers of the squadron, who, as occasion serves, give orders to the numbers in array and, the enemy approaching, to give an onset, certain of them be appointed to advance and maintain the receipt of them—whose discreet leading and valiant courage doth much comfort the rest to follow the same. These cavaliers be armed with corslets, and be placed in the heart of the battle, usually called the slaughter of the field or execution of the same, who commonly do not fight but in very great extremity.

389

ÆTATIS SVÆ 23
ANᵒ 1588

392 These our such new-fantasied men of war do despise and scorn our ancient arming of ourselves both on horseback and on foot, saying that we armed ourselves in times past with too much armour, or 'pieces of iron' as they term it. And therefore their foot-men piquers they do allow for very well armed when they wear their burgonets, their collars, their cuirasses and their backs without either pouldrons, vambraces, gauntlets or tasses.

393 The short sword, and sword and dagger, are perfect good weapons, and especially in service of the Prince. What a brave weapon is a short, sharp, light sword, to carry, to draw, to be nimble withal, to strike, to cut, to thrust both strong and quick! And what a goodly defence is a strong single hilt, when men are clustering and hurling together, especially where variety of weapons be, in their motions to defend the hand, head, face and bodies from blows—that shall be given sometimes with swords, sometimes with two-handed swords, battleaxes, halberds or black bills—and sometimes men shall be so near together that they shall have no space, scarce to use the blades of their swords below their waists; then their hilts (their hands being aloft) defendeth from the blows their hands, arms, heads, faces and bodies; then they lay on, having the use of blows and gripes, by force of their arms with their hilts, strong blows at the head, face, arms, bodies and shoulders, and many times, in hurling together, scope is given to turn down their points, with violent thrusts at their faces and bodies, by reason of the shortness of their blades, to the mighty annoyance, discomfort and great destruction of their enemies. One valiant man with a sword in his hand will do better service than ten Italians, or Italianated, with the rapiers.

These weapons the long bows are weapons of 394 singular advantage and effect for battles and great encounters, both against horsemen and footmen, and chiefly being so evil armed as all nations in these our days, both on horseback and on foot, are, because that the bow is a weapon wonderful ready in all seasons, both of fair and foul weather (which muskets and harquebuzes are not).

137

POSTVRES TO THE MVSKETTIER AND
PLAINLY EXPRESSED IN THE INSTRVCTIONS FOLLOWING.

Cap Bond

Cap Williams

Cap Style

Cap Smith

Cap Halsey

Cap Exley

Cap Spering

Cap Walton

Cap Milborn

Cap Peirton

If in marching you vnderstand oz perceiue that hozsemen will affault you, then place fiue pikes in ranke, and betwirt euerie pike a shot, so marching fozward, they fall to be ten ranke quadzant, placing your halberds and Enfigne in the midst.

A quadrant mixed with shot.

Likewise you may foz y defence of hozsemen, place ten ranks of pikes euerie way, your shot nert vnto this, your halberds and Enfigne in the midst, the pikes ends couched on the ground the better to defend the enimie.

A quadrant defending the shot.

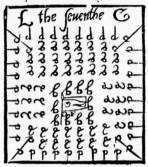

398 I must not forget nor cease to tell Her Majesty's good, wise, and gracious providings for us, her captains, and our soldiers, in summer heats and winter colds, in hunger and thirst, for our backs and our bellies: that is to say, every captain of an hundred footmen doth receive weekly, upon every Saturday, his full entertainment of twenty-eight shillings. In like case, every lieutenant fourteen shillings; an ensign, seven shillings; our sergeant, surgeon, drum and fife, five shillings pay, by way of imprest; and every common soldier, three shillings; delivered to all by the poll weekly. To the four last lower officers, two shillings weekly, and for every common soldier, twenty pence weekly, is to be answered to the full value thereof in good apparel of different

kinds, part for winter, and part for summer, which is ordered of good quality and stuff for the prices; patterns whereof must be sent to the Lord Deputy to be compared and prepared as followeth:

Apparel for an officer in winter

A cassock of broad cloth, with baize, and trimmed with silk lace, 27 shillings and 7 pence.

A doublet of canvas with silk buttons, and lined with white linen, 14 shillings and 5 pence.

Two shirts and two bands, 9 shillings and 6 pence.

Three pair of kersey stockings, at 2 shillings and 4 pence per pair, 7 shillings.

Three pair of shoes of neat's leather at 2 shillings and 4 pence per pair, 7 shillings.

One pair of Venetians, of broad Kentish cloth, with silver lace, 15 shillings and 4 pence.

In summer

Two shirts and bands, 9 shillings 6 pence.
Two pair of shoes, 4 shillings 8 pence.
One pair of stockings, 2 shillings 8 pence.
A felt hat and band, 5 shillings 5 pence.

399

A cassock of Kentish broad cloth, lined with cotton, and trimmed with buttons and loops, 17 shillings 6 pence.

A doublet of canvas with white linen lining, 12 shillings 6 pence.

A hat cap coloured, 7 shillings.

Two shirts of Osnabridge Holland and bands, 8 shillings.

Three pair of neat's leather shoes, 2 shillings 4 pence each, 7 shillings.

Three pair kersey stockings, 8 shillings.

One pair Venetians, of Kentish broad cloth, with buttons, loops and lining of linen, 13 shillings 4 pence.

In summer

Two shirts of Osnabridge and 2 falling Holland bands, 7 shillings.

Two pair neat's leather shoes, 4 shillings 8 pence.

One pair of stockings, 2 shillings 8 pence.

A hat cap coloured, 3 shillings.

Thus, friend Thomas, Her Majesty, with wonted grace, hath graced our bodies, and may heaven's grace clothe her in everlasting robes of righteousness, and 'on earth peace' to her who always sheweth 'good will toward all men'.

Alfo you may arme a Partezan, Iauelin, or Fork with fire-worke, to offend or defend a breach, fhip, or any place of defence, and to fhoot euery of them feuen or eight Piftol or Caliuer bullets; in nailing a plate of yrõ croffe the pike or point of the faid Iauelin, or betweene the graines of the Fork, piercing certain holes through the fame, ynto which with a ftrong wyer you may make faft on either fide fo many pipes of yrõ of 7. or 8. inches length as you think conuenient to fix vpõ either or any of the faid weapons; & charging the fame with powder, bullet, and wad, you may caufe the fame to fire one after another, in filling a role of canuas fewed together as the draught F. fheweth, with flow receit and coated as afore is taught, the which placed arteficially vpon the faid fhort barrels or pipes, as the draught G. H. fheweth, and primed with fine powder directly againft the touch-holes of the faid fhort barrels, pafting a little paper ouer the fame, firing the faid traines at both the

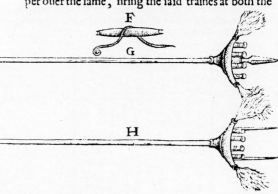

ends,

you fee a paire of compaffes, the armes or legs whereof are made in proportion to the blade of a knife, taper-wife, and bowing fharpe towardes the point as the draught hereunder fheweth, where the draught O. fheweth how the fame is to be put into the peece after the powder and wad, and the draught P, fheweth how the fame in his violent motion flieth through the ayre like a fith, being fhot out of any peece of great Ordinance.

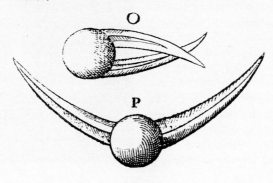

The Navy

FROM her sister, Elizabeth inherited a royal navy of but twenty-two warships over 100 tons, and of these most were not seaworthy. Fortunately, her inheritance from her subjects was a long tradition of adventure on the waves—a tradition which in her reign produced the living symbols of Hawkins, Raleigh and Drake.

Under the inspiration of Hawkins, the navy was slowly refashioned, partly by the proper fitting-out of older ships, partly by the building of new vessels, of which the 690-ton *Ark Royal* of 1587, designed to be manned by 268 mariners, 32 gunners and 100 soldiers, was the chief. The ancient lumbering form gave way to designs better calculated to offer the advantages of speed and manoeuvrability, so that the twenty-nine ships Elizabeth left to James in 1603 bore hardly any relation to those she took over from Mary.

The royal navy, however, was the least of England's sea-might in the sixteenth century. Elizabeth, characteristically economical in expenditure of state moneys and astute politically, found a solution in the encouragement of private enterprise. Numerous great vessels were constructed by venturers and many voyages of a bellicose nature were conducted without the placing of awkward responsibility on the Queen: she could easily repudiate what her captains had done even while gaining by an appropriation of part of the spoils.

Into perilous oceans the sea-hawks sailed. They followed the path taken by Sir Hugh Willoughby in 1553, northwards to Russia. They penetrated into the Levant, much to the annoyance of worthy Venetians. They braved the Atlantic and took delight in harassing Spanish galleons and Spanish treasure-forts. With Drake they sought even more hazardous journeys to the Pacific and, again with him, circumnavigated the globe. Still more significantly, they vaguely glimpsed the splendours of 'plantation', and, although the English colonies in America did not become firmly established until after Elizabeth's death, there were men in her reign who saw visions of a 'new Britannia' and a spreading empire. One of the united states bears proudly the name of the virgin queen.

It was because of these ships and their men, not simply because of a strengthened royal navy, that the massive Armada was broken, to become the prey of those lashing storms which the Elizabethans, confident of divine power and secure in their faith, unhesitatingly ascribed to the jealous wrath of God.

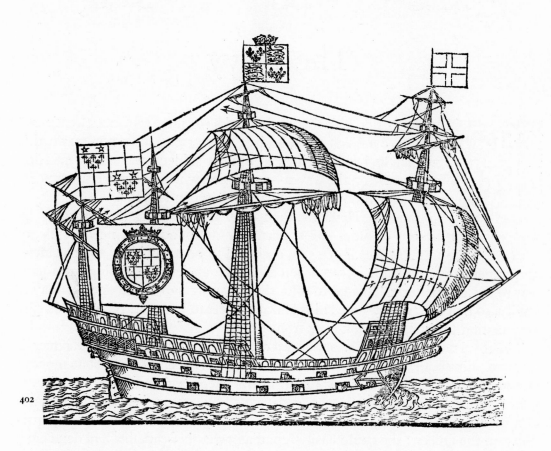

402

403 Whereas the Kings of England, down to Henry VII and Henry VIII, were wont to keep up a fleet of one hundred ships in full pay as a defence, now the Queen's ships do not amount to more than fifteen or sixteen, as her revenue cannot support a greater charge; and so the whole of the strength and repute of the nation rests on the vast number of small privateers, which are supported and increase to that dangerous extent which everyone recognises; and to ensure this support, the privateers make the ministers partners in the profits, without the risk of a penny in the fitting out, but only a share in the prizes, which are adjudged by judges placed there by the ministers themselves.

404 This Princess, being confident in these native sea-walls of ours, fit to bear moving bulwarks in martial times, and in civil traffics to carry out and in all commodities with advantage, she double

A͞n ᴼ · D͞Ñ͞I · 1571 ·
ÆTATIS · SVÆ
29 ·

Sir Richard Granville, killed
in a sea-fight near the Azores.
1591

143

pitch, resin, tar, masts, deal boards, cordage &c. for the building and maintaining of her navy, flourishing in multitude of ships for war and trade.

And as the life of that vast body she for increase of mariners gave princely countenance to all long voyages, knowing they would necessarily require ordnance, men, munition and burthen; and further to encourage this long-breathed work, she added out of her exchequer an allowance of so much in the ton for the builders of any ships upward of so many hundred tons; she cherished the fisher-boats with privileges along her coasts, as nurseries of seamen, brought Greenland and Newfoundland fishing in reputation to increase her stock of mariners, both by taking and transporting what they took far off.

The Queen's ships are being manned, but not without using the violence of the press-gang in seizing men in the streets of London to send them on board, whether they like it or no.

The wares that they carry out of the realm are for the most part broad cloths and kersies of all colours, likewise cottons, friezes, rugs, tin, wool, our best beer, baize, bustian, mockadoes (tufted and plain), rash, lead, fells, etc., which, being shipped at sundry ports of our coasts, are borne from thence into all quarters of the world and there either exchanged for other wares or ready money, to the great gain and commodity of our merchants. And whereas in times past their chief trade was into Spain, Portugal, France, Flanders, Dansk, Norway, Scotland and Iceland only, now in these days, as men not contented with these journeys, they have sought out the East and West Indies, and made now and then suspicious voyages, not only unto the Canaries and New Spain, but likewise into Cathaia, Moscovia and Tartaria, and the regions thereabout, from whence (as they say) they bring home great commodities.

stored her navy magazines with all materials, provided beforehand for such works and things as required time, and could not be bought with money; besides, she furnished her sea arsenals with all kind of staple provisions, as ordnance,

ÆTAT SVE 45

412

413 So Drake (divine Eliza's champion),
    Seizing upon a prey of Indian gold,
Meaning to ship it home to Albion,
    Ballasts his bark with treasures manifold—
    Which when the griev'd Iberians do behold,
They swarm in troops to take his prize away
And to disrob him of his gainèd prey.

A thousand hell-mouth'd cannons' deadly shot,
    A thousand rattling muskets' hail-stones fly,
Yet thousand deadly cannons hurt him not,
    Nor thousand rattling muskets reck'neth he,
    But still rebeats them all as eagerly—
And maugre all their beards brings home the
    spoil,
Riching Eliza and Eliza's soil.

The English are becoming absolute masters of 414
these waters. The English are not satisfied with
having absorbed Venetian trade in the West
entirely, but are devoting themselves to a similar
object in the Levant. They trade in their own
ships to the ports of Alexandria, Alexandretta,
and Smyrna and other Turkish cities in Asia
Minor, and in the Archipelago.

Nay, in the Indian's East and West again 415
    What great things men may with sea-forces do,
Not only in suppressing of the main
    But in possessing land and cities too,
    By undertakings of a Maiden Queen,
May as in models to the world be seen.

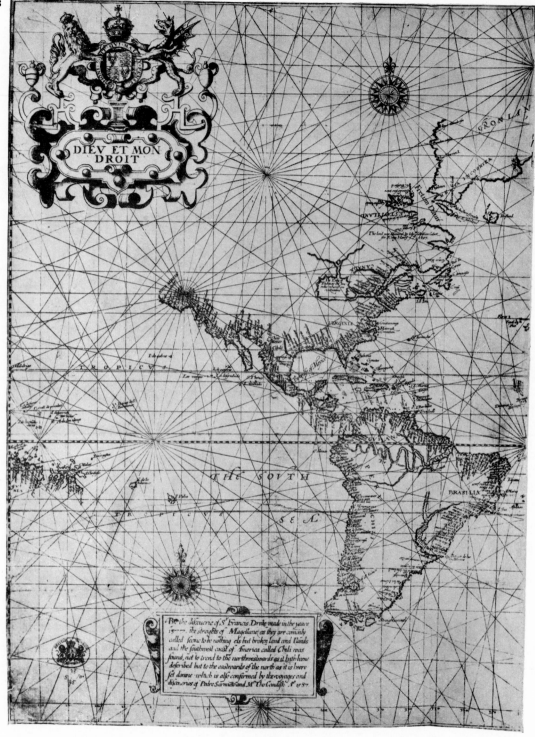

In this most famous and peerless government of her most excellent Majesty, her subjects, through the special assistance and blessing of God, in searching the most opposite corners and quarters of the world and, to speak plainly, in compassing the vast globe of the earth more than once, have excelled all the nations and people of the earth. For which of the kings of this land before Her Majesty had their banners ever seen in the Caspian sea? which of them hath ever dealt with the Emperor of Persia, as her Majesty hath done, and obtained for her merchants large and loving privileges? who ever saw before this regiment an English lieger in the stately porch of the Grand Signor at Constantinople? who ever found English consuls and agents at Tripolis in Syria, at Aleppo, at Babylon, at Balsara, and which is more, who ever heard of Englishmen at Goa before now? what English ships did heretofore ever anchor in the mighty river of Plate, pass and repass the unpassable (in former opinion) strait of Magellan, range along the coast of Chile, Peru and all the backside of Nova Hispania, further than any Christian ever passed, traverse the mighty breadth of the South sea, land upon the Luzones in despite of the enemy, enter into alliance, amity and traffic with the princes of the Moluccas and the isle of Java, double the Cape of Bona Speranza, arrive at the isle of Santa Helena and, last of all, return home most richly laden with the commodities of China, as the subjects of this now flourishing monarchy have done?

Fama:

421

NOTES

QUEEN ELIZABETH

The sixteenth century believed firmly in the seven-fold climacteric, and, if we are prepared to make some minor adjustments, Elizabeth's life may conveniently be thought of in seven-year spans. During the first seven years she found herself declared illegitimate—her mother, Anne Boleyn, having been hurried off to the block by her father, Henry VIII. At the age of fourteen (1547) her father died, and her half-brother came to the throne as Edward VI; immediately before she was about to welcome her twenty-first birthday (1554), his unfortunate death brought the crown to her fanatically Catholic half-sister Mary. For the next few years Elizabeth lived in imminent threat of execution: she did, indeed, suffer imprisonment at Woodstock and was even brought, in tears, to the Tower, but the grace of fortune, assisted by the skilful exercise of her own wits, held off the threatening danger until Mary died in 1558. For some time her seat on the throne remained precarious, becoming more or less assured only after the defeat of the Northern Rebellion in 1569, when she herself had just turned thirty-five. From this time on to 1588 (when she was approaching her fifty-sixth birthday) she succeeded in consolidating her position, although continually beset by dangers both at home and abroad. In 1587 the long-delayed execution of Mary Queen of Scots precipitated the sending forth of the great Spanish Armada, and its shattering by the guns of the little English ships and the mightier force of God's tempests brought with it a surge of patriotic sentiment, releasing other forces which had previously lain dormant. The Queen's grand climacteric, when the magic numbers seven and nine met in 1596 to give her sixty-three years of age, was passed in the very midst of that period (1590–1600) which forms for us our prime picture of the

153

'Elizabethan Age'. A new mood tends to enter in about 1600, an inescapable reaction, but certainly intensified both by the unfortunate Essex affair and by thoughts of the Queen's failing powers. Her death came in 1603, when the seven-year spans had reached their tenth revolution.

1. 'The Balance': detail from *Sir Thomas Chaloner* (National Portrait Gallery).

2. THOMAS HEYWOOD, Γυναικεῖον (1624), sig. A 2 verso. Thomas Heywood (c. 1570–1641) declared in 1633 that he was author or part-author of some 220 plays; but besides his activities as playwright and actor he found time for penning a number of other works, including two ambitious volumes of verse, *The hierarchie of the blessed angells* (1635) and Γυναικεῖον, in the latter of which he celebrated the stories of women famous in legendary and historical records.

3. JOHN NORDEN, *Vicissitudo rerum* (1600), stanzas 83, 97. The fame of John Norden (1548–1625?) rests mainly on his topographical work, *Speculum Britanniae* (1593, 1598), with its valuable maps and alphabetical list of towns and hamlets. Poetry, however, was part of the air the Elizabethans breathed, and we need not feel surprised to find this topographical-historical author producing a volume of verse, in which, characteristically, he turns to deal with a theme weighing heavily on many men's minds—the theme of mutability and constant change in human affairs.

4. 'The Queen's Pelican': detail from *Queen Elizabeth* (Walker Art Gallery, Liverpool). The pelican, a favourite symbol of Elizabeth, was the emblem of pious piety, the bird that fed its young from the flesh of its own breast. See 5, 7, 8, 14.

5. THOMAS DEKKER, *The pleasant comedie of Old Fortunatus* (1600), sig. A 1 verso. Dekker (1572?–1632?) was one of the most prolific playwrights and pamphleteers of the late sixteenth and early seventeenth centuries. The lines quoted here are from a 'Prologue at Court', specially written for the Queen herself. They well illustrate the ritual of adulation fostered by Elizabeth—an adulation which, however, must not be regarded as insincere. Elizabeth may have inspired such praise with political ends in view, but for Dekker and his companions she was indeed Pandora, the first of women and endowed with all the graces, Gloriana, the symbol of flourishing majesty, Cynthia, the image of maiden chastity, Belphoebe, the spirit of Diana, and Astræa, daughter of the gods and custodian of the scales of justice. See 4, 7, 8, 15, 47.

6. Paul Hentzner, account of a visit to England, 1598, in W. B. Rye, *England as seen by Foreigners* (1865), pp. 103–5.

7. *King Henry VIII and his Successors* (Mrs J. H. Dent-Brocklehurst, Sudeley Castle, Winchcombe). Philip and Mary, with Mars, are on the left; the boy Edward VI kneels at Henry's left, and Elizabeth comes forward with the figures of Peace and Plenty. The picture is inscribed:
'The Quene to Walsingham this Tablet sent
Mark of her Peoples and her owne Content.'
See 4, 5, 8, 14, 48.

8. 'The Queen's Virtues': detail from *Queen Elizabeth* (Dover Town Hall). See 4, 5, 7, 14, 48.

9. *Queen Elizabeth* (Capt. E. G. Spencer Churchill, Northwick Park).

10. Queen Elizabeth, speech on dissolving Parliament, 1601, in *The Journals of all the Parliaments during the reign of Queen Elizabeth*, collected by Sir Simonds D'Ewes, revised by Paul Bowes (1682), p. 659.

11. *The Black Book of Warwick*, transcribed and edited by Thomas Kemp (Warwick, 1898), p. 91. The 'Black Book' is an invaluable contemporary record of important affairs in Warwickshire.

12. JOHN NICHOLS, *The Progresses and Public Processions of Queen Elizabeth* (1823), III, 1–4. The extract given here presents merely a few of the items in the original list, and the entries have been simplified. The giving of presents at New Year was a custom eagerly maintained at court: Elizabeth herself gave presents in return to her entourage, but every year her treasury and her wardrobe must have been considerably the gainers. New Year's day for this and other purposes was, as now, 1 January, but considerable confusion could and did arise in this age from the fact that, by another reckoning, the old year closed on 24 March. Both dates were in common use. Thus a document dated, say, 20 January 1590 might either be what we mean by that date or else 20 January 1591. A further, and different, possibility of confusion arose from the fact that England did not follow the system of dating instituted in 1582 by Pope Gregory XIII and universal in at least the Catholic countries of the continent, by which ten days were dropped from the calendar. (This calendar was adopted in England only in 1752.) In the years with which

we are here concerned, an English visitor to France or Italy might well be expected to date a letter, say, 15 November 1590, which for his correspondent at home would be only 4 November.

Murrey = mulberry colour, purplish red; *safeguard* = outer dress worn to protect a woman's costume when riding; *sarcenet*, or *sarsenet* = a fine silk material.

13. *Queen Elizabeth*: illumination in the Queen's Bench Coram Rege Rolls, 1 Elizabeth, 1558 (Public Record Office).

14. *Queen Elizabeth and the Goddesses*, by Hans Eworth, 1569 (H.M. the Queen, Hampton Court). The allegorical intent here is in the story of the judgment of Paris—Elizabeth winning the prize from Juno, Venus and Pallas. There are inscribed verses:
'Juno potens sceptris et mentis acumine Pallas,
  Et roseo Veneris fulget in ore decus;
Adfuit Elizabeth, Juno perculsa refugit,
  Obstupuit Pallas erubuitque Venus.'
Before the Queen, Juno's majesty is cast down, wise Pallas stands dumb and Venus blushes for shame. See 4, 5, 7, 8, 48.

15. Sir John Harington, note c. 1594, in *Nugæ antiquæ*, ed. Henry Harington (1804), I, 170–1. Sir John Harington (1561–1612) was Elizabeth's godson, a lively and independently minded observer of characters and events. His own chief claims to fame are: (1) his translation of Ariosto's *Orlando Furioso* (1591), a work carried out at royal command; and (2) his invention of the water-closet, described in *The metamorphosis of Aiax* ('a jakes', 1596), for the writing of which Elizabeth, deeming its theme indelicate, banished him from her court.

16. Queen Elizabeth to the Lords and Commons, 1566: quoted from Cambridge University Library MS. G. g. III 34 in Sir John Neale, *Elizabeth I and her Parliaments* (1953), p. 149.

17. Sir John Harington to Robert Markham, 1606, in *Nugæ antiquæ*, ed. Henry Harington (1804), I, 355–62. See 15.

18. *Queen Elizabeth* (National Maritime Museum).

19. *Queen Elizabeth*, attributed to Marcus Gheeraerts the Younger, 1592 (National Portrait Gallery). Gheeraerts (1561–1635) came with his father to England and painted many portraits.

20. *Queen Elizabeth* (Capt. E. G. Spencer Churchill, Northwick Park).

21. Sir John Harington to Robert Markham, 1606, in *Nugæ antiquæ*, ed. Henry Harington (1804), I, 355–62. See 15.

22. FULKE GREVILLE, *The Life of Sir Philip Sidney* (1652), ed. Nowell Smith (Oxford, 1907), pp. 175–6, 186–7. Born about 1554, Fulke Greville became a favoured courtier of the Queen; eventually he was knighted (1597) and raised by James I to the peerage as Baron Brooke (1621). During moments of leisure from his political duties he applied himself enthusiastically to the writing of lyrics and academic dramas, although for the most part these works remained unpublished during his life-time. In thus combining courtly activities with the pursuit of literature he associated himself with the activities of his school-mate, Sir Philip Sidney, to whom and to whose memory he was fondly devoted. It is not known when Greville wrote his life of Sidney, but probably this was some fifteen years before his own death in 1628. See 59.

23. *Queen Elizabeth* (Lord Methuen, Corsham).

24. NICHOLAS BRETON, 'In praise of Queen Elizabeth', British Museum MS. 6207, fols. 16 verso–17 verso. This encomium was no doubt penned immediately after the Queen's death. Breton seems to have been born about 1545 and lived on to about 1626. He was a prolific author of pamphlets in prose and verse, animated by a peculiar and pleasing admixture of trenchant realism and romantic sentiment.

25. 'The Queen's Hand': detail from *Queen Elizabeth* (Duke of Bedford, Woburn Abbey).

26. THOMAS DEKKER, *The wonderfull yeare* (1604), sig. B 4 recto. The wonderful year was 1603, when Elizabeth died, James I came to the throne of a united England and Scotland, and one of the most terrible visitations of the plague descended upon the country. See 5.

27. WILLIAM BOURNE, *A regiment for the sea* (1574), sig. M 3 recto.

28. THOMAS BLUNDEVILE, *M. Blvndeuile his exercises* (1594), fol. 181 recto. Note should be taken of the characteristic way in which nearly all men rejected the theories of Copernicus. The tendency was to cling to the Ptolemaic system, whether, as some said, that had eleven spheres or, as others averred, ten or only nine.

29. *Ibid.* fols. 135 recto–136 recto. See 28.

30. *Ibid.* fol. 156 recto and verso. See 28.

31. WILLIAM CUNNINGHAM, *The cosmographical glasse* (1559), title-page.

32. THOMAS BLUNDEVILE, *M. Blvndeuile his exercises* (1594), fol. 156 recto and verso. See 28.

33. CHRISTOPHER MARLOWE, *The tragicall history of D. Faustus* (acted about 1588, first printed 1604), ed. F. S. Boas (1932), p. 92. Next to Shakespeare, Marlowe (1564–93) was unquestionably the greatest dramatic poet of the sixteenth century, and his popularity in the theatre is shown by the dozens of references to his works, particularly *Tamburlaine the Great* (1590). Like Shakespeare, he also won fame for his narrative verse, *Hero and Leander* (written before 1593, printed 1598) finding much praise and many imitators.

34. Sir PHILIP SIDNEY, *Sir P.S. his Astrophel and Stella* (written *c.* 1582, printed 1591), sonnet xxvi, sig. B 3 recto. Regarded as the ideal Elizabethan gentleman, Sidney (1554–86) won the whole-hearted admiration of his age. A man of action, he was a poet of high distinction; his *Apologie for poetry* (1595) was the best critical work of the time; and *The Countesse of Pembroke's Arcadia* (1590) proved an influence on many dramatists and others. When he died at the battle of Zutphen, the esteem in which he was held was shown by his vast elaborate funeral and by the mourning verses written on the occasion. See 22, 59, 381, 387.

35. MICHAEL DRAYTON, *Endimion and Phoebe* (1595), sigs. E 3 verso–E 4 recto. Drayton (*c.* 1563–1631) during his long career applied himself both to drama and poetry; most of his plays are lost, but there has come down to us a mighty volume of lyrics, narrative and descriptive poems. His contemporary and later fame rests largely on his verses celebrating episodes in older English history and upon his 'chorographicall description of Great Britain', *Poly-Olbion* (1612). See 371.

36. JOHN DEE, *The elements of geometrie* (1570), sig. biii recto and verso. Elizabethan England had many astrologers, but none was so well-known as Dee (1527–1608), Elizabeth's own protégé. During an adventurous life in England and abroad in which, while holding various posts in holy orders, he gained highest esteem as a mathematician, effected medical cures, claimed to have discovered the philosopher's stone and to have familiar conference with spirits, he moved from acclaim in court and academic circles to a poverty-stricken old age.

37. Sir WALTER RALEIGH, *The history of the world* (1614), pp. 12–14. Brilliant and adventure-some, Raleigh (1552?–1618) was in a sense his own worst enemy. His handsome figure, his daring exploits and his literary attainments gave him the qualifications for high court preferment; but he shared too freely in the arrogant passion of his age. During Elizabeth's reign he ran foul of Essex, and during the reign of James his enemies succeeded in bringing him to execution. A great voyager, he was responsible for several important expeditions to the New World; he had the vision of colonization in these lands; at the time of the Armada he proved one of the most valiant of the Queen's naval commanders; he produced in his *History* one of the great prose-writings of the period; he was an independent and original thinker who surrounded himself with several 'scientists' of the age; and, in addition, he was a poet of no mean distinction. See 411.

38. Astrolabe, made by R. Melbourne, 1631 (Science Museum).

39. RICHARD GRAFTON, *A briefe treatise containing many proper tables* (1599), pp. 90–4. Grafton (d. 1572?), publisher and author, is known chiefly for his concern with the printing of the Bible in English and for his *Chronicles of England* (1562, 1568). His *Briefe treatise*, which appeared originally in 1571 or before as *A litle treatise*, is a typical Elizabethan compendium of information chronological and astrological.

40. 'Celestial Chart': engraving by Benjamin Wright, in John Blagrave, *Astrolabium uranicum generale* (1596), The author of this work was described shortly after his death in 1611 as 'the flower of mathematicians of his age'.

41. THOMAS HILL, *The schoole of skil* (1599), sigs. A 4 verso–A 5 recto. Hill was a typical Elizabethan 'scientist', author of a diversity of works on 'vulgar arithmetic', gardening, physiognomy, 'the contemplation of mankind' and 'the most pleasaunte arte of the interpretacion of dreames'.

42. 'The Eleven Heavens and the Four Elements': engraving in Andrew Borde, *The fyrst boke of the introduction of knowledge* (1542), sig. A 4 verso. Starting his career as a monk, and later suffragan Bishop of Chichester, Borde (1490?–1549) turned in 1528 to study medicine abroad. Serving for a time at Glasgow University (where he did not like the Scots), he later discovered a kind of spiritual home at Montpellier. A cheery, racy character, he wrote on matters medical, astronomical and astrological; he was responsible for sending the first rhubarb seeds to England; and to him were attributed at least three books of 'merry tales' and jests. The chart given here well illustrates the contemporary concept of correspondences. Beneath the Moon is the mutable world of the Elements, and each of the 'Heavens' has its attached qualities. Jupiter, for example, is hot and moist, benevolent, and is represented among the metals by tin. See 39, 47.

43. MICHAEL DRAYTON, *Endimion and Phoebe* (1595), sig. E 3 verso. See 35, 371.

44. NICHOLAS BRETON, *Wits trenchmour* (1597), sig. C 3 verso. See 24.

45. TIMOTHY BRIGHT, *A treatise of melancholie* (1586), pp. 4–5. Melancholy was the 'humour' most prevalent and most feared in this age, and many are the descriptions of its fatal effects when allowed to grow unchecked. Bright (1551?–1615) in this work anticipates the great *Anatomy of melancholy* (1621) by Robert Burton. In the course of an adventurous life, during which he experienced the horrors of the St Bartholomew Massacre at Paris in 1572, he travelled widely; eventually he took holy orders. Among his other activities he was one of the inventors of shorthand: his *Characterie: an arte of shorte, swifte and secret writing* (1588) was dedicated to the Queen. It should be noted that, while there was general agreement about the natures of the four humours, much confusion and inconsistency reigned among those who sought to explain the psychological effects of these humours in conjunction. Despite such confusion and inconsistency, however, the whole of medical practice was based on this concept, men's actions were explained by their humours, and Ben Jonson founded his principles of dramatic portraiture on them.

46. Sir WALTER RALEIGH, *The history of the world* (1614), pp. 25–6. See 37, 411.

47. 'A Sphere of Correspondences': woodcut on title-page of Robert Anton, *The philosophers satyrs* (1616). Here another set of correspondences is graphically presented. Thus Taurus, Virgo and Capricornus are connected with the Moon, Water, the East Wind, Autumn, Middle-age and the Phlegmatic humour. See 42.

48. 'Queen Elizabeth and the Spheres': woodcut in J. Case, *Sphaera civitatis* (1588?), p. 61. Case (d. 1600) spent most of his energies on the interpretation of Aristotle: all his works are in Latin. He was successively Fellow of St John's, Oxford, Canon of Salisbury, and practising doctor. See 4, 5, 7, 8, 14, 42, 47.

49. SAMUEL PURCHAS, *Purchas his pilgrim. Microcosmus or the historie of man* (1619), pp. 117, 119–20. The career of Purchas (1575?–1626) was a peculiar one. An avid traveller, his most famous work is his *Pilgrimage* (1613), a record of his adventures. In later life he settled down as Rector of St Martin's, Ludgate; holding to the title of his original book, at this time he produced his moral-philosophical *Pilgrim* besides a later *Pilgrimes* (1625). *Samplar* = sampler or example; *vive* = lively, living.

50. JOHN WYLKINSON, *The ethiques of Aristotle* (1547), sig. A 6 recto and verso.

51. RICHARD HOOKER, *Of the lawes of ecclesiasticall politie* (1594–7), p. 57. The prime 'apology' of the Anglican church, Hooker's vast study is both a masterpiece of Elizabethan prose and an important philosophical document. Hooker (1554?–1600) never attained high office, but he was in close association with many of the chief ecclesiastics of his time.

52. *Young man in red*, c. 1550 (H.M. the Queen, Hampton Court).

53. Sir THOMAS SMYTH, *De repvblica anglorvm* (1583), p. 86. Smyth (1513–77) wrote his work on Tudor government from active experience. He was Secretary of State in 1548 and 1572, besides serving on divers occasions as royal ambassador. *Hault* = proud, haughty.

54. FYNES MORYSON, *An itinerary* (1617), Book III, ch. i, p. 28. [Cited hereafter as MORYSON]. Moryson (1566–1630) was an indefatigable and restless traveller. He toured through the whole of Europe and the Middle East, producing in his *Itinerary* an invaluable record of these various countries.

55. WILLIAM HARRISON, 'The description of Britaine', in Raphael Holinshed, *The first and second volumes of the chronicles* (1587), p. 199. [Cited hereafter as HARRISON]. By far the most popular history of England was that produced by Raphael Holinshed (1578 and 1587), a work which served Shakespeare as the main source for his histories. The author of the 'Description of Britaine', included in these chronicles, Harrison (1535–93), was in holy orders and became Canon of Windsor in 1586.

56. Paul Hentzner, account of visit to England, 1598, in W. B. Rye, *England as seen by Foreigners* (1865), p. 110.

57. *Cyuile and vncyuile life* (1579), sigs. E 3 recto–F 2 verso.

58. *Margaret Duchess of Norfolk*, by Hans Eworth (Lord Braybrooke, Mutlow Hall).

59. *Sir Philip Sidney* (National Portrait Gallery). See 22, 34, 381, 387.

60. *Robert Devereux, Earl of Essex* (National Portrait Gallery). Next to the Queen, Essex (1567–1601) was perhaps the most colourful character of the period. After the death of the Earl of Leicester in 1588, he assumed a prime position at court; but, impetuous and inclined to flamboyance, he steadily ruined his fortunes by a series of imprudent actions culminating in the disastrous 'rebellion' which forced Elizabeth to agree to his execution.

61. HARRISON, p. 164. *Mails* = travelling bags. See 55.

62. Emanuel van Meteren, account of visit to England, 1599, in W. B. Rye, *England as seen by Foreigners* (1865), p. 70.

63. JOHN LYLY, *Euphues and his England* (1581), fol. 112 recto and verso. Lyly (1554?–1606) was the first of the greater Elizabethan dramatists, producing a series of mythological-allegorical comedies between 1584 and 1590. In his own time, however, he was best known for his *Euphues* (1578), in which he developed a peculiar kind of writing, replete with similes from what has been called 'unnatural natural history' and with artificial use of antithesis: the style created a vogue at court and soon many were trying to talk in the new 'Euphuistic' manner. *Euphues and his England*, first printed in 1580, is a sequel following up his initial success. In addition to writing for the stage he was for several years master of one of the companies of child actors.

64. LEVINUS LEMNIUS, *The touchstone of complexions*, translated by Thomas Newton (1581), fol. 48 recto. This work was originally published in 1565.

65. Paul Hentzner, account of visit to England, 1598, in W. B. Rye, *England as seen by Foreigners* (1865), pp. 110–11. See 352–9, 361, 414.

66. HARRISON, p. 156. See 55.

67. Sir WALTER RALEIGH, *The history of the world* (1614), sigs. B 3 verso–B 4 recto. The general concept of harmony in the universe, whence came the music of the spheres, embraced also the natural world, including the world of man. Thus the idea of 'degree', by which everything and everyone was placed in a particular position, was of prime import in this age. Any breaking of degree, no matter how trivial, could and did create confusion far beyond its own area. A clear statement of this philosophy is given by Ulysses in *Troilus and Cressida*, while *Macbeth* shows how one individual crime disturbs the whole of nature. See 37, 411.

68. PHILIP STUBBES, *The anatomie of abuses* (1583), sig. C 2 recto and verso. Stubbes was a puritan prose-writer and versifier whose downright and effective style in this work and in *A christal glasse for Christian women* (1591) brought him wide popularity. See 67, 69.

69. MORYSON, Book III, ch. iv, p. 179. See 54.

70. HARRISON, p. 172. *Almaine* = German; *Morisco* = Moorish; *polled* = cut short; *weaselbecked* = sharp-nosed or sharp-featured. See 55, 79.

71. PHILIP STUBBES, *The anatomie of abuses* (1583), sigs. D 6 verso–E 3 recto. *Sarcenet* or sarsenet = a fine silk material; *paned* = made with strips of cloth; *canions* = rolls of material at the bottom of breeches. See 68.

72. I.M., *A health to the gentlemanly profession of seruingmen* (1598), sig. H 2 verso.

73. *The Black Book of Warwick*, transcribed and edited by Thomas Kemp (Warwick, 1898), pp. 35–6. This refers to a visit by Leicester in 1571. See 11, 74.

74. *Robert Dudley, Earl of Leicester* (National Portrait Gallery). Before the advent of Essex, Leicester (1532–88) was the most prominent of Elizabeth's favourites, by some thought likely to become her husband. The scandal surrounding the death of his wife, Amy Robsart, in 1560 seriously threatened the good name of the Queen herself.

75. *Henry Wriothesley, Earl of Southampton* (Duke of Portland). Internal evidence suggests that this picture was painted while Southampton (1573–1624) was imprisoned in the Tower because of his complicity in the Essex rebellion. A distinguished representative of a family ennobled by Henry VIII, he became prominent at court and proved a notable patron of letters: to him Shakespeare dedicated his poems in 1593 and 1594. His marriage to Elizabeth Vernon, Essex's cousin, in 1598, brought the Queen's anger upon him, and that anger was intensified when he appeared as one of Essex's supporters in the abortive 'rebellion'. Imprisoned in 1601, he languished precariously in the Tower until James I released him in 1603. Note may be taken of the cat in this picture: pet dogs frequently were painted with their masters or mistresses, but the appearance of a pet cat is rare, if not unique. See 60.

76. E. GUILPIN, *Skialetheia* (1598), epigram 53, sig. B 4 recto. *Slop* = breeches; *dag cases* = cases for pistols; *Cad's beard* = (apparently) Cadiz beard.

77. ROBERT GREENE, *A qvip for an vpstart covrtier* (1592), sig. H 1 verso. Greene (1558–92) was typical of many young intellectuals of his age. After taking his degrees in 1578 and 1583, he sought to make a living by his pen, applying himself to the drama and, more particularly, to the topical pamphlet. Exploiting the current interest in rogues and sharpers, his name became associated with a series of 'conycatching' booklets in which he exposed the tricks of the underworld (the sort of thing that nowadays might form articles for the popular illustrated weeklies or the more sensational dailies). All his manifold activities, however, could not keep pace with his reckless living, and he died on a pauper's bed, leaving behind him his *Groats-worth of witte* (1592), famous for its allusions to Shakespeare. *Applesquire* = pimp; *murrey-cloth* = purple-coloured cloth; *camerard* = comrade; *watchet* = light blue.

78. THOMAS NASHE, *Pierce Penilesse his supplication to the diuell* (1592), sig. A 3 verso. Another but somewhat less unfortunate dramatist and pamphleteer, Nashe (1567–1601?) left Cambridge about 1588, and thereafter issued a long series of topical and controversial booklets, exhibiting a racy style and keenly observant eye. *Slops* = breeches; *budge* = fur.

79. 'The Puzzled Englishman': woodcut in Thomas Harman, *A caueat or warening for common cvrsetors* (1567), fol. 14 verso. The Englishman, naked, stands with cloth and shears, uncertain what the cut of his clothes shall be. See 69.

80. THOMAS NASHE, *Purse Penilesse his supplication to the diuell* (1592), sig. B 3 verso. *Canaries* = a Spanish dance. See 78.

81. *Sir Edward Hoby*, 1578 (Miss P. Vansittart Neale, Bisham Abbey). The son of Sir Thomas Hoby, remembered for his translation of Castiglione's *Cortegiano*, Sir Edward Hoby (1560–1617) pursued a parliamentary, political and scholarly career which associated him with most of the men prominent in his time. His mother was Elizabeth, daughter of Sir Anthony Cooke and sister of Lady Burghley and Lady Bacon; he himself married Margaret Carey, daughter of Lord Hunsdon, cousin to the Queen and holder of many important posts. See 84.

82. ROBERT GREENE, *A qvip for an vpstart covrtier* (1592), sig. D 2 recto and verso. *Coventry* = blue thread and cloth. See 77.

83. *Greenes vision* (1592), sig. D 2 recto. *Russeted* = trimmed with russet-coloured cloth; *kersey* = a coarse woollen cloth; *tagged welt* = border made of strips of material or slashed; *slop* = breeches; *stock* = stocking; *lockram* = linen material; *Coventry* = blue thread.

84. *Anne Fitzwilliam, later Lady Cooke*, 1585 (Duke of Bedford, Woburn Abbey). Wife of Sir Anthony Cooke, this lady was the grandmother of Sir Edward Hoby. Her three daughters were esteemed among the most cultured and intellectual women of their time. See 81.

85. *Greenes vision* (1592), sig. D 2 recto and verso. *Stomacher* = waistcoat or covering for the breast; *mockado* = a very popular kind of cloth; *partlet* = neckerchief or ruff; *holland* = a linen material; *whip* = overcast stitch.

86. *Lady Kytson*, by George Gower, 1573 (Tate Gallery). Lady Kytson was the wife of Sir Thomas Kytson. Gower, the artist, was the first distinguished native English painter. In 1584 he was granted a patent whereby he and Nicholas Hilliard had a monopoly in making portraits of the Queen. See 364.

87. *Sir Christopher Hatton*, ascribed to Cornelis Ketel, 1582 (Winchelsea Settled Estates). Born a simple country squire, Hatton (1540–91) attracted Elizabeth's attention, characteristically, by his grace of figure and, it is said, by his skill in dancing. The Queen, however, was not one to allow her sentiments to rule her reason, and Hatton's promotions were due to his own sterling abilities. For some years he acted as her spokesman to the House of Commons; the extent of his interests is shown by his distinguished governmental services and by his wide patronage of writers and of artists, among whom was the Dutchman Cornelis Ketel (1548–1616), who worked in England from 1573 to 1581 or 1582.

88. *Mary Sidney, Countess of Pembroke* (Lord De L'Isle and Dudley, Penshurst Place). See 344.

89. Early seventeenth-century gloves (Victoria and Albert Museum).

90. *Progress of Queen Elizabeth to the Palace of Nonsuch*, by Joris Hoefnagel (British Museum). Hoefnagel was a Dutchman who came for a short time to England about 1569. Nonsuch, or Nonesuch, Palace, situated near Sheen in Surrey, became one of the Queen's favourite residences.

91. *Procession of Queen Elizabeth to Blackfriars,
9 June 1600*, attributed to Marcus Gheeraerts the
Younger (Simon Wingfield Digby, Esq., Sher-
borne). The occasion was the marriage of Lady
Anne Russell to Lord Herbert. To the left, the
first man is probably Lord Howard de Walden,
later the Earl of Suffolk, Constable of the Tower;
the man in a skull-cap is the Earl of Nottingham,
Lord High Admiral; next to him is his brother-in-
law, George Carey, Lord Hunsdon, Lord Chamberlain; next (with the state sword) Henry
Brooke, Lord Cobham, Warden of the Cinque
Ports. Bearing the left pole of the chair of state,
at the rear, is Lord Herbert, the bridegroom,
who points to his future wife; in front of him is
Edward Russell, Earl of Bedford, his brother-in-
law; the bald-headed man facing forwards is the
Earl of Worcester, his father; at the front of the
pole is, probably, Lord Herbert of Cardiff. The
other pole has, as front bearer, Roger Manners,
Earl of Rutland. The lady to the left of the bride
is her mother, Lady Russell, and to her left is
Lucy Harington, wife of Edward Russell. The
men guarding the road are Yeomen of the Guard
and Gentlemen Pensioners.

92. 'A Civic Procession': part of an engraving,
Civitatis Londini (1600), by John Norden (Royal
Library, Stockholm). See 3.

93. Sir THOMAS SMYTH, *De repvblica anglorvm*
(1583), pp. 33–4, 43–7. 'The Queen absolute'
at l. 6 does not mean that the Queen had complete
authority; it refers simply to times when the
throne is held by a queen in her own right. See
53.

94. *William Cecil, Lord Burghley* (Burrell Collection, Glasgow). Cecil (1520–98) became
Secretary of State in 1550, and Elizabeth, when
she ascended the throne, wisely continued him
in his post. To him, more than to any other, the
Queen was indebted for the wise direction of
her policy, internal and foreign. He was an
untiring civil servant and it is clear that for him
the Queen had an abiding affection.

95. *Thomas Radcliffe, Earl of Sussex* (National
Portrait Gallery). Like Sir Henry Sidney, the
Earl of Sussex (1526?–83) spent much of his time
in Ireland, where he was Lord Deputy from 1556
to 1564. He was active in trying to persuade
Elizabeth to marry a foreign prince, and because
of this he ran foul of the Earl of Leicester.

96. John Lyly, *Euphues and his England* (1581),
fol. 112 verso. See 63.

97. HARRISON, p. 196. See 55.

98. NICHOLAS BRETON, 'Necessary notes for a
courtier', appended to *The court and country*
(1618), in *Inedited Tracts* (Roxburghe Library,
1863), p. 207. See 24.

99. *Sir Henry Sidney*, 1573 (National Portrait
Gallery). Much of Sidney's (1529–86) active
career was taken up with affairs in Ireland. His
work was marked by his devotion to his public
duties, although in the end he incurred Elizabeth's
anger because of his large expenditure of money
there.

100. ANTHONY MUNDY, 'The woodman's walk',
in *Englands Helicon* (1600), sig. Aa 3 verso. This
book was one of the several anthologies of poetry
which appeared during Elizabeth's reign. Mundy
(*c.* 1553–1633) had a long and interesting career
as lyric-writer, balladist, playwright, pamphleteer
and minor man-of-affairs. In his youth he
travelled to Rome and made use of what he saw
there in attacks on the Jesuits, even securing
a position as pursuivant for the execution of
warrants against recusants. Later he became a
frequent contributor of material for Lord Mayor's
pageants.

101. BEN JONSON, GEORGE CHAPMAN and JOHN
MARSTON, *Eastward Hoe* (1605), sig. C 1 recto.
Collaboration in the writing of plays was very
common in these times: occasionally this may
have involved close discussion and joint penning
of entire works; more commonly perhaps, it
amounted to no more than the working-out of
a plot, followed by a sharing-out of the individual
scenes. Here, three well-known poets are associated. Jonson (1572–1637) came to be regarded
as a kind of dramatist arbiter in the seventeenth
century; Chapman (*c.* 1560–1634), besides his
plays, won a measure of immortality for his
translation of Homer; Marston (*c.* 1575–1634),
after an early career as verse satirist, theatre-man
and playwright, ended his life decorously in holy
orders.

102. *Sir Nicholas Bacon*, 1579 (National Portrait
Gallery). Nicholas Bacon (1509–79), father of
Francis, was Lord Keeper of the Great Seal from
1558 to 1579. He was an active associate of Lord
Burghley and, like him, an industrious civil
servant. See 376.

103. *William Paulet, Marquis of Winchester and
Earl of Wiltshire* (National Portrait Gallery).
After considerable service under Henry VIII,
Paulet (1485?–1572) gained the favour of Eliza-
beth. He was Lord Treasurer from 1550 to 1572.

104. *Elizabeth Hardwick, Countess of Shrewsbury*
(National Portrait Gallery). Known as 'Bess of

Hardwick', Elizabeth Hardwick (1518–1608) amassed enormous wealth through inheriting the estates of four husbands. Her passion was for building and she was responsible both for Chatsworth and Hardwick House. In 1569 she and her husband were entrusted with the custody of Mary Queen of Scots. See 267.

105. *The Somerset House Conference*, 1604 (National Portrait Gallery). On the left are the foreign envoys. On the right, Robert, Lord Cecil (son of Lord Burghley); Henry Howard, Earl of Northampton; Charles Blunt, Earl of Devonshire; Charles Howard, Earl of Nottingham; and Thomas Sackville, Earl of Dorset. The tapestries are dated on the border 1560.

106. *Lord William Russell of Thornhaugh*, 1588 (Duke of Bedford, Woburn Abbey). Lord Deputy of Ireland from 1594 to 1597, Russell (1558?–1613) pursued an active military career. He fought at Zutphen with Sir Philip Sidney, who bequeathed him his armour, and for a time he acted as Governor of Flushing. See 59.

107. Sir THOMAS SMYTH, *De repvblica anglorvm* (1583), pp. 34, 35–6. See 53.

108. JOHN STOW, *A svrvay of London* (1598), pp. 387–92. One of the most important antiquaries of his time, Stow (1525?–1605) was responsible for the *Annals of England* (1592 and later) and *A Svrvay of London* (1598 and later): these have made him a prime authority on the events of Elizabeth's reign and on London topography. The courts were of great importance to men of this time since their passionate temper made Elizabethans naturally litigious and the changing economic conditions necessitated the bringing of many cases before the judges. Of particular importance was the Court of Chancery where in especial the principle of equity, the application of 'natural law' (some might have called it 'common sense'), was considered alongside the application of the laws of the land, and where the Queen's prerogative applied.

109. *Sir John Doderidge* (National Portrait Gallery). Doderidge (1555–1628) was a distinguished lawyer and judge.

110. *Sir Roger Manwood* (National Portrait Gallery). Although a noted lawyer and judge, Manwood (1525–92) was several times under suspicion of corrupt practices, chiefly the taking of bribes.

111. HARRISON, p. 180. See 55.

112. JOHN TAYLOR, 'Wit and Mirth', in *All the workes of John Taylor* (1630), pp. 180–1. Called 'the water poet', Taylor (1580–1653) spent a varied and frolicking career as naval seaman, Thames waterman, traveller and versifier. Befriended by the Jonson group, he acquired wide notoriety, and his adventures (including an attempt to sail from London to Queensbrough in a brown-paper boat) were a familiar topic of conversation.

113. BARNABE RICH, *The honestie of this age* (1614), sig. B 4 recto and verso. Soldier and author, Rich (1540?–1617), published a long line of miscellaneous writings, of which one, *Riche his farewell to militarie profession* (1581), was known and used by Shakespeare. There is plentiful evidence that numbers of minor lawyers, or pettifoggers, deliberately toured the country for the purpose of exciting quarrels and so of encouraging men to take their cases to the courts.

114. *The Court of Wards and Liveries* (Duke of Richmond and Gordon). The man at the head of the table is probably Lord Burghley, who was Master of the Court from the beginning of Elizabeth's reign until 1598. On the left come (apparently) the Chief Justice of the King's Bench; Thomas Seckford, the Surveyor from 1580 to 1589; George Goring, the Receiver-General; and Marmaduke Servant, the Usher. On the left are the Chief Justice of Common Pleas; Richard Kingsmill, an attorney; William Tooke, the Auditor. The two figures in the front are the sergeants Thomas Gent and Edmund Anderson.

115. THOMAS DEKKER, *The seven deadly sinnes of London* (1606), sig. F 3 verso. Of the London prisons (leaving the Tower aside) the most important were Newgate (sometimes called 'Whittington's College', because of the money given to it by Dick Whittington), Ludgate, the Fleet, and the Counters in Wood-street, the Poultry and Southwark. In general, these prisons were operated in a manner strange to us. The governor was a leaseholder of the building, and his income derived from the fees paid by prisoners. Erected round quadrangles, the four parts came to be known as 'sides'; a man with money could fare well, even luxuriously, if he could afford to be in the 'master's side', but for those in the poorer quarters life was a misery. Sometimes their only chance of obtaining food was from the pennies placed by the charitable in pleading hands thrust up from the 'hole' or other gratings, or from the donations of bread gathered by one of their number as he trudged, basket on back, seeking alms in the streets. It must be borne in mind that the importance of the prisons then was very great, since a far higher proportion than now of London's citizens suffered incarceration. If, for instance, we look at the lives of the dramatists active between 1590 and 1610, it is hard to find one except Shakespeare for whom we have not evidence of a longer or shorter prison term, or who had not to flee from impending arrest. See 5, 119.

116. WILLIAM FENNOR, 'The compters commonwealth', in *A trve description of the lawes, ivstice, and eqvity of a compter* (1629), sigs. B 2 verso–B 3 verso.

117. *Sir Thomas Fleming*, 1596 (National Portrait Gallery). Called to the bar in 1577, Fleming (1544-1613) held many important legal posts and eventually was made Chief Justice of the King's Bench in 1607.

118. WILLIAM BURTON, *The rowsing of the slvggard* (1595), p. 44. Burton (d. 1616), noted as a vigorous preacher, was of the puritan persuasion; his sermons and other writings display keen observation and an effective style. See 119.

119. 'Begging Bread for the Prisoners', in *The manner of crying things in London* (? 1600). This collection of prints exists in a unique copy in the Henry E. Huntington Library: it is conjecturally put in 1600 because a work of this kind was entered in the Stationers' Register on May 16, 1599, but the costumes suggest a slightly later date. See 118.

120. HARRISON, p. 185. See 55.

121. HARRISON, p. 184.

122. 'A Prison': print on title-page of *The life, apprehension, arraignement, and execution of Charles Courtney* (1612). This is a kind of composite picture, showing both an attempted escape and the fatal ends of two malefactors.

123. Sir THOMAS SMYTH, *De repvblica anglorvm* (1583), p. 85. See 53.

124. 'Hands in prayer': detail from portrait said to be of Richard Hooker (National Portrait Gallery). See 5.

125. JOHN LYLY, *Euphues and his England* (1581), fol. 110 recto and verso. See 63.

126. THOMAS TYMME, *A plaine discouerie of ten English lepers* (1592), sig. D 3 verso. Rector of St Antholin in London, Tymme (d. 1620) was the author of an enormously popular work called *A silver watch-bell* (1605), besides various other pious and moral writings.

127. *Archbishop Matthew Parker* (Corpus Christi, Cambridge). Parker (1504–75) was Archbishop of Canterbury from 1559 to 1575. A deeply learned prelate and a cultured patron of the arts, he was largely responsible for directing the course of the Anglican Church between the extremes of Roman Catholicism and Puritanism.

128. *Archbishop John Whitgift* (National Portrait Gallery). In 1577 Whitgift (1530?–1604) was appointed Bishop of Worcester and in 1583 became Archbishop of Canterbury. An opponent of the Puritans, he was the main object of attack in the notorious 'Martin Marprelate' pamphlets.

129. *2 Return from Parnassus* (acted 1602), in *The three Parnassus Plays*, ed. J. B. Leishman (1949), pp. 263–4. The 'Parnassus' plays were academic pieces, with a strong satirical flavour; and they give a good picture of the efforts of the young intellectual in his struggle to make a living.

130. *John Foxe* (Trinity Hospital, Guildford). Famous as the author of the *Actes and monuments* (1563), a record of the lives of the anti-Roman martyrs, Foxe (1516–87) was an active adherent of the Knox persuasion.

131. NICHOLAS BRETON, *Pasqvils mad-cap* (1600), sig. B 2 verso. See 24.

132. NICHOLAS BRETON, *A merrie dialogve betwixt the taker and mistaker* (1603), pp. 12–13. See 24.

133. London Bridge: engraving by C. J. Visscher (1616). See 136.

134. THOMAS DEKKER, *The seuen deadly sinnes of London* (1606), sig. C 2 recto. Towards the latter part of Elizabeth's reign London's population numbered about 200,000, more than twelve times more than any other town in the kingdom. The streets were narrow and awkward, and hence the Thames was much more used than now for all kinds of traffic: it was the river, too, which mainly bound together the two cities of London and Westminster, the former the mercantile centre and the latter the centre of court and governmental activities. See 5.

135. JOHN LYLY, *Euphues and his England* (1581), fol. 109 verso. See 63.

136. MORYSON, Book III, ch. ii, pp. 64–5. The most usual manner of crossing from London to Southwark was by boat, and presumably most of the theatre-goers attending performances of Shakespeare's plays at the Globe journeyed in this manner. See 54, 133.

137. JOHN STOW, *A svrvay of London* (1598), p. 11. See 108.

138. MORYSON, Book III, ch. ii, p. 64. See 54, 145, 315.

139. MORYSON, Book III, ch. ii, p. 69. See 54.

140. 'London and Westminster': drawing by William Smith in *The particuler description of England* (1588), Sloane MS. 2596 (British Museum).

141. *Cyuile and vncyuile life* (1579), sig. L 4 recto.

142. BARNABE RICH, *The honestie of this age* (1614), sig. B 4 recto. Elizabethan shops were for the most part open to the street like booths, and many allusions show that the owners or their apprentices stood outside attracting customers by a reiterated 'What do you lack?' See 113, 198.

143. MORYSON, Book III, ch. ii, p. 65. See 54.

144. JOHN STOW, *A svrvay of London* (1598), pp. 62–3. See 108.

145. 'The Royal Exchange': engraving attributed to Franciscus Hogenberg, *c.* 1596. The Royal Exchange was built by Sir Thomas Gresham in 1566. The engraver, Franciscus Hogenberg, a German, worked in England from about 1572–87. See 138, 315.

146. JOHN STOW, *A svrvay of London* (ed. 1603), pp. 84–5. Coaches did not become a menace to London's streets until the end of the sixteenth century, but contemporaries make it quite clear that the menace, in the narrow inconvenient streets, was a real one. See 108.

147. E. GUILPIN, *Skialetheia* (1598), satire 5, sigs. D 4 recto–D 5 verso.

148. *Preaching at Paul's Cross* (Society of Antiquaries). The open-air sermons delivered weekly at Paul's Cross were important affairs, and frequently the government made use of them by instructing the preachers to deal (in an approved manner) with certain current issues.

149. JOHN EARLE, *Micro-cosmographie* (1628), essay 53, sig. I 11 recto. Paul's Walk was in the precincts of the old cathedral, and was noted as a place wherein gallants might show off their new clothes, country visitors might be accosted by rogues, servants might be hired and bills might be set up on the pillars. This was the place, too, frequented by impoverished gentlemen, who hung about hoping that someone might invite them for a meal. Since a prominent monument in the cathedral was Duke Humphrey's tomb, it was a common saying that those who were not

lucky in their search for a free meal 'dined with Duke Humphrey'. Earle (1601?–65), after a long career in the church, eventually became Bishop of Worcester in 1652.

150. THOMAS DEKKER, *The dead tearme* (1608), sigs. D 4 verso–E 1 recto. *Gull* = dupe; *apple-squire* = pimp. See 5.

151. E. GUILPIN, *Skialetheia* (1598), satire 5, sigs. D 5 verso–D 7 recto. *Puisnes* = youngsters.

152. 'The Ratcatcher': print accompanying a ballad, *The famous Ratketcher, with his trauels into France, and of his returne to London* (?1615).

153. THOMAS DEKKER, *The guls horne-booke* (1609), sigs. D 3 verso–D 4 recto. The 'ordinary' was an inn with a fixed charge for a meal, and one receives the impression that the atmosphere was more similar to that of a modern French café than to that of an English restaurant. Individual ordinaries had their own peculiar clienteles, so that one was the haunt of poets, another of merchants, another of gallants. The reference to 'publish your clothes' alludes to the fact that Paul's Churchyard was the chief centre of the book trade. See 5, 149.

154. 'Steel and tinder-box', in *The manner of crying things in London* (?1600). See 119.

155. BARNABE RICH, *The honestie of this age* (1614), sig. D 4 recto and verso. Tobacco seems to have been first brought to England about 1565, taken up as a fashion at court (possibly inspired by the example of Raleigh) and thence carried to humbler surroundings. It was not, however, until the reign of James, himself the author of *A counter blaste to tobacco* (1604) that the question of smoking became a live, and hotly-debated, issue. See 113.

156. WILLIAM SHAKESPEARE, *The comedy of errors* (acted about 1593 or earlier), I, ii, 97.

157. 'Fresh cheese and cream', in *The manner of crying things in London* (?1600). See 119.

158. *The groundworke of conny-catching* (1592), leaf 2 verso. Although perhaps Robert Greene and his companions, in their search for copy, may have exaggerated somewhat, there seems to be no doubt that London was overrun with tricksters. Playwrights as well as pamphleteers give many examples of their devices; picking of pockets or cutting of purses appears to have been a common hazard for all playgoers. Many plays, too, give examples of a common trick by which usurers, in making a loan, insisted that a considerable part should be supplied, not in money, but in largely worthless goods. Many needy young men were caught in this way—among them, the poet and dramatist George Chapman.

159. 'London Porters': print accompanying Thomas Brewer, *A newe Ballad, composed in commendation of the Societie, or Companie of Porters*. According to this, there were 'a thousand fortie one' porters in London, who formed a Corporation on the model of other city companies.

160. 'The Bellman': woodcut on title-page of Thomas Dekker, *The belman of London* (1608). The bellman, walking London's streets at night, was a familiar figure, and many pamphleteers used him as a symbol warning the city of its errors. See 5.

161. William Fleetwood to Lord Burghley (Lansdowne MSS. no. 44, art. 38), in A. Ellis, *Original Letters* (1824), II, 295–302. Fleetwood (1535?–94) was Recorder of the City of London.

162. THOMAS DEKKER, *The belman of London* (1608), sig. I 1 recto. *Inquinations* = defilements. See 5, 160.

163. ANTHONY MUNDY, 'The woodman's walk' in *Englands Helicon* (1600), sig. A a 4 recto. See 100.

164. 'A Brothel': woodcut fontispiece to N. Goodman, *Hollands Leaguer* (1632). The brothels in the suburbs were notorious. Many of them seem to have had armed guards at their gates and their arboured gardens were notorious.

165. 'The Bull- and Bear-baiting Rings': detail from a map of London in Georg Braun and Franciscus Hogenberg, *Civitatis orbis terrarum* (1574). See 145.

166. *The Swan Theatre, c.* 1596: drawing after Johannes de Witt (Universiteitsbibliotheek, Utrecht). This is the only contemporary representation of the interior of an Elizabethan playhouse.

167. THOMAS DEKKER, *The dead tearme* (1608), sig. B 3 recto. See 5.

168. Lupold von Wedel, account of visit to England, 1585, in Victor von Klarwill, *Queen Elizabeth and some Foreigners*, translated by T. H. Nash (1928), p. 315.

169. Sir JOHN DAVIES, *Epigrammes and elegies* (1590?), sig. D 2 recto and verso. *Muted* = besmeared; *Plowden, Dyer and Brooke* = standard legal text books (E. Plowden, *Les comentaries, ou les reportes de dyuers cases* (1571) and many later editions); Sir James Dyer, *Cy ensuont ascuns nouel cases* (1585) and other works; Sir Robert Brook or Brooke, *Ascuns novell cases* (1578 and many later editions); legal affairs still called for the use of bastard Norman-French; *Harry Hunks and Sacarson* = famous bears of the time (the latter referred to by Slander in *The merry wives of Windsor*). See 165, 167.

170. THOMAS DEKKER, *Worke for armorours* (1609), sig. B 1 verso. See 5.

171. T. WHITE, *A sermon preached at Pawles Crosse on Sunday the thirde of Nouember 1577* (1578), sigs. C 7 verso–C 8 recto. White (1550?–1624) had a distinguished ecclesiastical career and, by his will, established Sion College in London. The 'common plays' were those presented publicly by the companies of adult actors who, to escape being classed as 'rogues and vagabonds', were theoretically at least in the service of a lord; thus Shakespeare's company was the Lord Chamberlain's Men. Besides the performances given by such companies, there were performances presented by companies of children, who attracted particular esteem shortly after 1600 and whose activities are referred to in *Hamlet*. It should be remembered also that amateur playing was fairly widespread: schools and colleges frequently put on comedies, sometimes in Latin but also in English; on occasion, members of the Inns of Court similarly amused themselves; and it seems probable that there were more performances in certain noble houses than we might have thought. Outside of London, strolling companies carried plays to the more important market-towns, and, especially in time of plague, even great actors such as Alleyn took to the roads. In London, the typical theatres used by the adult actors were of the form illustrated in the drawing of the Swan; the first of these, The Theatre, was erected in 1576 and the most famous, The Globe, in 1599. These were all situated outside the city boundaries because of opposition by the civic authorities, either eastwards of the old walls or across the river in Southwark. The children performed in smaller indoor houses, generally called 'private' theatres. In addition, inn-yards, which had been the actors' original haunts, and halls were put to theatrical service. See 148.

172. JOHN STOCKWOOD, *A sermon preached at Paules Cross* (1578), pp. 23–4, sigs. B 8 recto and verso. Stockwood (d. 1610), a well-known preacher and one-time head of Tonbridge school, has a fairly long list of pious and educational writings, most of them marked by vigour and almost puritanical flavour. The blowing of a trumpet was the recognized sign that a play was about to be performed. See 148.

173. Sir John Harington, 'A treatise on playe', *c.* 1597, in *Nugae antiquae*, ed. Henry Harington (1804) I, 191. Throughout this period the playing of Latin and occasionally English comedies written by academic authors was a custom well-established at Oxford and Cambridge. See 15.

174. RICHARD BRATHWAIT, *The English gentleman* (1630), sig. B b 3 recto. Brathwait (1588?–1673) was a minor poet and prose writer in the Greene tradition. Besides his *English gentleman*, his best-known work is *Barnabees journall* (1638): all his writings have a racy quality.

175. Pipe and tabor: part of woodcut on title-page of Robert Greene, *The honorable historie of Frier Bacon and Frier Bongay* (1630 edition). See 77.

176. STEPHEN GOSSON, *The schoole of abuse* (1579), sig. C 1 verso. Starting as a poet, play-wright and player, Gosson (1554–1624) turned later to attack the stage. That he maintained contact with old friends, even after he became a worthy and serious-minded rector, is shown by the fact that in 1616 he was styling the actor Alleyn as his 'very loving and ancient friend'. *Foot-saunt* is in reference to a popular card game called saunt.

177. THOMAS DEKKER, *The guls horne-booke* (1609), sig. E 2 recto. In Elizabethan times the man who sought to make a living from his pen naturally turned to the stage, since it offered, in general, higher pecuniary rewards than did the publishing houses. A well-established play-wright might expect from £6 to £10 for a play. See 5.

178. GEORGE CHAPMAN, *Eugenia* (1614), sigs. F 1 verso–F 2 recto. The passage is important as testifying to the intent silence in the theatres despite the motley nature of the audience. See 101.

179. THOMAS DEKKER, *If it be not good, the diuel is in it* (1612), sig. A 4 verso. This is one of the few contemporary critical pronouncements on the reception of plays. The emphasis is obviously on the charming power of verse melody and on the arousing of emotions. See 5.

180. ROBERT GREENE, *Greenes, Groats-worth of witte* (1592), sigs. D 4 recto and verso. Obviously this is autobiographical and gives a general picture of the way in which the young Greene, just down from the university, started to write for the stage. It may be noted that in Elizabethan theatres,

which had no scenery, large sums were spent on elaborate costumes. On occasion, a single dress might cost more than the payment given to the playwright. *Conster* = construe, interpret. See 77.

181. *Richard Burbage* (Dulwich College). Apart from Alleyn, Burbage (1567?–1619) was the most famous tragic actor of his age. He was one of Shakespeare's 'fellows' and almost certainly 'created' the chief characters in his mature dramas.

182. THOMAS DEKKER, *Iests to make you merie* (1607), in *The non-dramatic works of Thomas Dekker*, ed. A. B. Grosart (1885), II, 303. See 5.

183. *Nathaniel Field* (Dulwich College). Nat Field (1587–1633), dramatist as well as actor, won his reputation in the children's companies which became the rage during the early years of the seventeenth century.

184. Act of the Common Council, 6 December 1574 (*Malone Society Collections*, I, 2 (1908), p. 175, from Lansdowne MSS.).

185. THOMAS DEKKER, *Worke for armorours* (1609), sig. B 1 recto. See 5.

186. THOMAS DEKKER, *The wonderfull yeare* (1604), sig. C 3 recto and verso. See 5.

187. THOMAS COGAN, *The haven of health* (1584), pp. 274–5. A doctor and schoolmaster, Cogan (1545?–1607) spent most of his life in Manchester; he was head of the Grammar School there from 1574 to 1600. The various herbs mentioned here are listed in Gerard's *Herball* as preventatives of the plague; *setwall*, or valerian, was so particularly thought of that there was a popular rime—

> 'They that will have their hale
> Must put setwall in their kale'.

Elecampane was a tonic plant, good also for shortness of breath and 'an old cough'.

188. Orders in time of plague, *c.* 1593 (*Malone Society Collections*, I, 2 (1908), pp. 206–10, from Lansdowne MSS.).

189. MAURICE KYFFIN, *The blessednes of Brytaine* (1587), sig. A 4 recto. Except for traders' tokens, sixteenth-century coins were made of gold or silver. Up to 1601 the sovereign was usually valued at 30s. and, in addition to coins familiar to us, there were angels or nobles (value from about 6 to 10 shillings), groats (value 4d.) as well as smaller silver coins, 2d., 1½d., and three farthings. Frequently calculations were made in marks (value 13s. 4d.). It is almost impossible to equate the buying-power of Elizabethan money with present-day money; some staple commodities were very cheap but others seem to us now alarmingly dear; for convenience, and with all due caution, a multiplier of 10 or 20 may be used. See 190.

190. Elizabethan sovereign of thirty shillings of standard gold coinage (enlarged) (Fitzwilliam Museum, Cambridge). See 189.

191. MICHAEL DRAYTON, *Poly-Olbion* (1613), 'illustrations' to song xiii, p. 223. See 35, 371.

192. THOMAS DEKKER, *The belman of London* (1608), sigs. B 1 verso, E 1 verso. See 5.

193. ANTHONY MUNDY, 'The woodman's walk', in *Englands Helicon* (1600), sig. Aa 4 recto and verso. The reading 'untruly' is taken from the second edition, 1614: the first reads 'soothly'. See 100.

194. 'Country Toils and Pleasures': detail from a sixteenth-century tapestry (Victoria and Albert Museum).

195. WILLIAM VAUGHAN, *The golden-groue* (1600), sig. T 4 recto and verso. Vaughan (1577–1641) is as typical as any of his age. After leaving Oxford in 1597, he travelled widely in Europe and later was responsible for establishing a colony in Newfoundland. As an author, his works range from religious tracts, moral pamphlets, writings on the New World and controversial pamphlets to his *Naturall and artificiall directions for health* (1600), a book often reprinted.

196. *Cyuile and vncyuile life* (1597), sigs. B 2 verso–B 3 recto. *Countries* = counties or country districts.

197. WILLIAM VAUGHAN, *The golden-groue* (1600), sigs. P 7 recto–P 8 recto. See 195.

198. *Marriage fête at Bermondsey*, by Joris Hoefnagel, 1590 (Marquess of Salisbury, Hatfield House). In the distance is the Thames, with the Tower on its further bank. Note should be taken of (1) the man and his wife, with panniers, on the left, (2) the shop in the middle foreground, (3) the banquet spread in the shop on the right. See 142.

199. I.M., *A health to the gentlemanly profession of seruingmen* (1598), sigs. G 4 recto–H 1 recto. *Cypher in augrim* = zero, cypher in algorism or Arabic, i.e. 0.

200. GEORGE GASCOIGNE, *The steele glas* (1576), sig D 3 verso. Minor poet, courtier, soldier, Gascoigne (*c.* 1535–77) was the stepfather of Nicholas Breton. His chief importance rests in his introduction of Ariosto's *I suppositi* to England.

201. THOMAS NASHE, *The anatomie of absurditie* (1589), sig. C 4 verso. See 78.

202. 'Rochester': drawing by William Smith in *The particuler description of England* (1588), Sloane MS. 2596 (British Museum).

203. NICHOLAS BRETON, *Wits trenchmour* (1597), sig. E 2 verso. See 24.

204. Privy Council proclamation, 10 March 1594, in E. Arber, *An English Garner* (1877), I, 301–2. *Grassing* = grazing.

205. I.M., *A health to the gentlemanly profession of seruingmen* (1598), sig. H 2 recto and verso.

206. Sir JOHN FERNE, *The blazon of gentrie* (1586), pp. 21–2.

207. HARRISON, p. 203. See 55.

208. 'Canterbury': drawing by William Smith in *The particuler description of England* (1588), Sloane MS. 2596 (British Museum). This drawing gives an excellent view of the typical walled town of Elizabethan times.

209. 'Country Scene': sixteenth-century cushion cover (Victoria and Albert Museum).

210. NICHOLAS BRETON, *The court and country* (1618), in *Inedited tracts* (Roxburghe Library, 1868), p. 183. *Checking* = choking, losing breath. See 24.

211. 'Hunter and Hawk': woodcut on title-page of George Turbervile, *The booke of faulconrie* (1575). Among the early poets of the reign, Turbervile (1540?–1610?) had an interesting career which even took him to Russia in 1568. Besides his work on falconry he has a collection of miscellaneous verses and translations from Ovid and Italian authors.

212. *Cyuile and vncyuile life* (1579), sigs. H 3 verso–H 4 recto. Unfortunately not as much as could be wished is known about Elizabethan games. Cards, dice and backgammon were all very popular, and stakes seem, in general, to have run high. All the books mentioned are, characteristically, of older vintage, those which had become popular among the countryfolk. The romance of *Guy of Warwick* had been printed before 1500, as had that of *The Four Sons of Aymon*; *The Ship of Fools*, translated from Sebastian Brant by Alexander Barclay, was issued in 1509; *A Hundred Merry Tales* came about 1525; this and *The Book of Riddles* are mentioned by Shakespeare. Thérouanne and Tournai appear in the original as 'Turryn and Tornay': these were engagements in 1513.

213. 'Queen Elizabeth at the Hunt': woodcut in George Turbervile, *The booke of faulconrie* (1575), p. 112. See 24.

214. *James I as a Boy, with a Hawk* (Scottish National Portrait Gallery).

215. SAMUEL ROWLANDS, *The letting of hvmovrs blood in the head-vaine* (1600) sigs. D 6 verso–E 1 recto. In a sense, Rowlands (1570?–1630?) may be regarded as a successor to Greene and Dekker. His numerous writings, mostly of a topical kind, contain much interesting material on various aspects of life in the early seventeenth century. *Loggats* = a game where sticks are thrown at a mark; *nine-holes* = a game played with small balls.

216. WILLIAM SHAKESPEARE, *The taming of the shrew* (acted in 1594 or earlier). Induction, 41.

217. BEN JONSON, *Every man in his humor* (acted in 1598), in *The workes of Beniamin Jonson* (1616), p. 5. See 101.

218. GEORGE TURBERVILE, *The booke of faulconrie* (1575), sig. B 1 verso. *Mountee* = a technical term of the hawk's flight. See 211.

219. *Cyuile and vncyuile life* (1579), sig. H 3 recto.

220. W. DARELL, *A short discourse of the life of seruingmen* (1578), sig. F 4 recto.

221. GODFREY GOODMAN, *The fall of man* (1616), pp. 147–8. Goodman (1583–1656), a divine who became Bishop of Gloucester in 1625, was typical of the High Anglicans who, while conforming, secretly inclined towards the Roman Church.

222. MORYSON, Book III, ch. ii, pp. 61–2. See 54.

223. MICHAEL DRAYTON and others, *Sir John Old-castle* (1600), sig. C 2 recto. See 35, 371.

224. HARRISON, p. 199. *Dags* = large pistols; *snapper* = small pistol; *hanger* = sword; *capcase* = travelling bag. See 55.

225. MORYSON, Book III, ch. ii, p. 61. See 54.

226. *Ibid.* Book III, ch. iii, p. 151. See 54.

227. *Ibid.* Book III, ch. ii, p. 61. See 54.

228. LEVINUS LEMNIUS, *The touchstone of complexions*, translated by Thomas Newton (1581), fol. 48 recto. See 64.

229. 'Claudius Holliband' (i.e. Claude Desainliens), *The Italian school-maister* (1597), sig. B 8 recto.

230. THOMAS HILL, *A briefe and pleasaunt treatise entituled: Naturall and artificiall conclu-*sions (1581), sig C 2 recto. Besides the value of lupines and coliander (or coriander) for killing fleas, both herbs were currently recommended for destroying 'worms in the belly'; coloquintida was a purgative and was also supposed to be a cure for 'singing in the ears'. See 41.

231. Contemporary manuscript note in the Huntington Library copy of 230.

232. 'Four Beggars': woodcut on title-page of John Taylor, *The praise of Beggery* (1621). See 112.

233. THOMAS HARMAN, *A caueat or warening for commen cvrsetors* (1567), sig. A 2 recto.

234. *Ibid.*

235. THOMAS DEKKER, *The belman of London* (1608), sig. B 4 verso. See 5.

236. THOMAS DEKKER, *Lanthorne and candle-light* (1609), sig. B 4 verso. See 5.

237. JOHN AWDELEY, *The fraternitye of vacabondes* (1575), sig. A 2 recto and verso. Awdeley was a printer, ballad-writer and pamphleteer, flourishing from the beginning of Elizabeth's reign until 1577.

238. THOMAS DEKKER?, *O per se O* (1612), sig. L 2 verso. See 5.

239. THOMAS DEKKER?, *O per se O* (1612), sigs. L 3 verso–L 4 verso.

240. 'Robin Goodfellow and the Fairies': woodcut in *Robin Goodfellow: his mad prankes and merry jests* (1628), and used also for some ballads.

241. MICHAEL DRAYTON, 'Nimphidia: The court of fayrie', in *Poems* (1619), sig. Q 1 recto. See 35, 371.

242. REGINALD SCOT, *The discouerie of witchcraft* (1584), pp. 152–3. An M.P. in 1588, Scot (?1538–99) was one of the more enlightened of his age and his book on witchcraft was designed to aid those innocents who might be wrongly accused of association with the devil. His work was known and used by Shakespeare.

243. REGINALD SCOT, *ibid.* p. 131. See 242.

244. Jacob Rathgeb, account of visit to England by Frederick duke of Württemberg, 1592, in W. B. Rye, *England as seen by Foreigners* (1865), p. 50.

245. 'Witches and their Familiars': woodcut in Matthew Hopkins, *The Discovery of Witches* (1647).

246. GEORGE GIFFORD, *A dialogve concerning witches and witchcraftes* (1593), sig. B 1 recto. Gifford (d. 1620) was a well-known non-conformist and author of many theological works. His attitude towards witches is eminently common-sense, but he does not deny their existence.

247. 'Three Witches': print accompanying a ballad, *Damnable practises of three Lincoln-shire witches* (1619).

248. 'Design for a House': architectural drawing by John Thorpe (Soane Museum). Thorpe was one of the most active architects in England between 1570 and 1610, many great mansions being created from his plans.

249. THOMAS HILL, *The proffitable arte of gardening* (1568), sig. F 1 recto. See 41.

250. FRANCIS BACON, *The essayes* (1625), essay 45, sig. L l 1 recto. See 376.

251. ANDREW BORDE, *A compendious regiment or dietarie of health* (1576), sig. B 1 recto and verso. See 42.

252. HARRISON, p. 188. See 55.

253. ROBERT GREENE, *A qvip for an vpstart covrtier* (1592), sig. F 4 recto. See 77.

254. *Aston Hall.* Although not strictly Elizabethan, being built in the early seventeenth century, Aston Hall is an excellent example of the mansions which were arising in England from 1570 onwards. It was erected by Sir Thomas Holte (1571–1654). See 257, 258, 260.

255. THOMAS DEKKER, *A strange horse-race* (1613), sig. A 3 recto. See 5.

256. HARRISON, p. 187. See 55.

257. *Long Gallery, Aston Hall.* See 254.

258. *Staircase, Aston Hall.* See 254.

259. HARRISON, p. 188. *Geson* or *geason* = rare, extraordinary. See 55.

260. *A Panelled Room, Aston Hall.* See 254.

261. HARRISON, p. 188. See 55.

262. *Henry Stuart, Lord Darnley and his Brother Charles,* 1562 (H.M. the Queen, Palace of Holyroodhouse). After Mary Queen of Scots, Darnley (1545–67) was next in the line of accession to the throne of England. Married to Mary in 1565, he was murdered in 1567. Note should be taken of the bare character of the hall.

263. *The Great Bed of Ware* (Victoria and Albert Museum). This enormous bed, constructed in the early sixteenth century, was sufficiently proverbial by Shakespeare's time to find mention in *Twelfth Night*.

264. *Lucretia's banquet*: table carpet (Victoria and Albert Museum). 'Carpet' regularly signified 'cover' in the sixteenth century; the floors were usually strewn with rushes.

265. Oak coffer, *c.* 1600 (Victoria and Albert Museum).

266. Oak joint-stool, *c.* 1600 (Victoria and Albert Museum).

267. Inventory of Hardwick Hall, 1601. This inventory was made for 'Bess of Hardwick', the Countess of Shrewsbury. *Paned* = made of or ornamented with strips of cloth; *sparver* = canopy over a bed; *portals* = ornamental screens; *fustians* = blankets made of fustian; *sarcenet* = a fine silk material. See 104.

268. Oak armchair, early seventeenth century (Victoria and Albert Museum).

269. HARRISON, p. 188. *Treen* = made of wood. See 55.

270. Chased silver dish, London hallmark 1573–4 (Victoria and Albert Museum).

271. The 'Glynne' Standing Cup, from Hawarden Castle; silver-gilt with London hallmark 1579–80 (H. N. Gladstone, Esq.; Victoria and Albert Museum).

272. Lupold von Wedel, account of visit to England, 1585, in Victor von Klarwill, *Queen Elizabeth and some Foreigners*, translated by T. H. Nash (1928), p. 342.

273. HARRISON, p. 167. See 55.

274. Tigerware jugs mounted in silver, 1564 (Burrell Collection, Glasgow).

275. HARRISON, p. 209. *Laistowes* = rubbish heaps. See 55.

276. MORYSON, Book III, ch. iv, pp. 178–9. See 54.

277. Standing bell salt, 1603 (Burrell Collection, Glasgow). Large 'salts' were used at long tables to divide the more honoured guests from humbler retainers.

278. 'Of Diuels bit': from John Gerard, *The herball* (1597), p. 587. Among Elizabethan herbalists, Gerard (1545–1612) is the most prominent. A botanist and barber-surgeon, he made his great folio into an epitome of information on plants and their uses; his own garden in London was extensively stocked, and he was responsible for the laying-out and cultivation of the noted gardens of Lord Burghley.

279. RICHARD SMYTH, dedicatory sonnet in Henry Constable, *Diana* (1594) sig. A 2 verso.

One of the more important minor poets of the time, Constable (1562–1616) was an ardent Catholic and spent much of his time abroad in exile.

280. EDMUND SPENSER, '*An hymne in honovr of loue*' in *Fowre hymnes* (1596), pp. 7–8. The greatest non-dramatic poet of the Elizabethan period, Spenser (1552?–99) spent his life partly in government and court service, partly in the pursuit of literature. His vast narrative-allegorical *Faerie Queene* appeared in 1590, but already he was regarded by the younger litterateurs as a master; his *Shepheardes calender* had been printed fully twelve years before, in 1579.

281. NICHOLAS LING, *Politeuphuia. Wits common wealth* (1598), fol. 15 recto.

282. *Barbara Gamage, Countess of Leicester, and her Children*, by Marcus Gheeraerts the Younger, 1596 (Lord De L'Isle and Dudley, Penshurst Place). Barbara Gamage was the wife of Robert Sidney, Earl of Leicester. Praised in verse by Ben Jonson for her wifely virtues, she had a family of ten children. See 21.

283. ROBERT CLEAVER, *A godlie forme of hovsehold government* (1598), p. 358.

284. ROBERT CLEAVER, *ibid.* p. 15.

285. WILLIAM VAUGHAN, *The golden-groue* (1600), sigs. N 4 recto–N 5 verso. See 195.

286. Emanuel van Meteren, account of visit to England, 1575, in W. B. Rye, *England as seen by Foreigners* (1865), pp. 72–3.

287. Title-page of Charles Gibbon, *A work worth the reading* (1591).

288. ROBERT CLEAVER, *A godlie forme of hovseholde gouernment* (1598), pp. 279–82.

289. WILLIAM VAUGHAN, *The golden-groue* (1600), sig. V 8 recto. See 195.

290. 'A Wedding Feast': detail from *Sir Henry Unton* (National Portrait Gallery). Note should be taken of (1) the rear table with its array of silver, (2) the guests with their hats on, (3) the masque of children and (4) the consort of music.

291. HARRISON, p. 171. See 55.

292. JOHN LYLY, *Euphues and his England* (1581), fol. 111 recto. See 63.

293. THOMAS NASHE, *Pierce Penilesse his svpplication to the diuell* (1592), sig. E 2 recto and verso. See 78.

294. MORYSON, Book III, ch. iii, p. 150. See 54.

295. THOMAS DAWSON, *The good huswifes iewell* (1596), sig. A 2 recto. This popular work appeared originally in 1587.

296. 'The Making of Rosewater', from Conrad Gesner, *The treasure of Euonymas: conteyning the secretes of nature* (1559), p. 38. Gesner was a Swiss naturalist and chemist (1516–65), many of whose numerous works were well known in England.

297. MORYSON, Book III, ch. iii, p. 149. See 54.

298. THOMAS COGAN, *The haven of health* (1584), p. 139.

299. Privy Council proclamation, 10 March 1594, in E. Arber, *An English Garner* (1877), I, 301. *Expense* = consumption.

300. ANDREW BORDE, *A compendious regiment or dietarie of health* (1576), sigs. G 3 recto–G 5 recto. See 42. *Rere* = lightly cooked.

301. THOMAS DAWSON, *The good huswifes iewell* (1596), sigs. A 6 recto–C 6 recto. See 295.

302. Rosewater Ewer, with London hallmark 1583 (Victoria and Albert Museum). Since hardly anyone used forks, the use of ewers and basins at meals was a necessity.

303. THOMAS NASHE, *Pierce Penilesse his svpplication to the diuell* (1592), sig. E 4 recto. See 78.

304. *The weakest goeth to the wall* (1600), sig. B 2 recto.

305. HARRISON, p. 202. See 55.

306. MORYSON, Book III, ch. iii, p. 152. See 54.

307. MORYSON, Book III, ch. i, p. 31. See 54.

308. 'A Class-room': woodcut accompanying a ballad, *A table of good nurture* (from *The Roxburghe Ballads*, ed. W. Chappell, II (1874), 573).

309. RICHARD MULCASTER, *Positions* (1581), p. 229. Mulcaster (1530?–1611) was one of the foremost educationalists of his period: he was headmaster of Merchant Taylors' School from 1561 to 1586 and high master of St Paul's from 1596 to 1608.

310. Account attributed to Archbishop Laud, *c.* 1617, descriptive of conditions about 1600, in F. H. Forshall, *Westminster School* (1884), pp. 415–17.

311. HENRY PEACHAM, *The compleat gentleman* (1634), p. 27. Schoolmaster, amateur artist, mathematician, composer, expert in heraldry, Peacham (1576?–1643?) was well equipped to write of the qualities ideally called for from the contemporary gentleman. His numerous other writings include a treatise on 'limning', a discussion of the merits of coaches and sedans and writings on heraldry.

312. Timetable of the young Earl of Oxford (Public Records Office, SPD, Eliz. xxvi, 50).

313. Middle Temple Hall.

314. Sir Henry Sidney, letter to his son Philip, then at school at Shrewsbury, 1566, in *Letters and memorials of state*, ed. Arthur Collins (1746) I, 8–9. The boy was to become Sir Philip Sidney. See 99.

315. *Sir Thomas Gresham* (National Portrait Gallery). Gresham (1519?–79) became one of the richest merchants in London and aided materially in developing English trade. He built the Royal Exchange (1566–8), and laid the foundation of a university for London by establishing Gresham College. See 138, 145, 318.

316. HARRISON, p. 148. See 55.

317. HARRISON, p. 150. See 55.

318. JOHN STOW, *A svrvay of London* (ed. 1603), pp. 76–7. See 108, 315.

319. John Taylor, 'Wit and mirth', in *All the workes of John Taylor* (1630), p. 197. See 112.

320. NICHOLAS BRETON, *Pasqvils mad-cap* (1600), sig. E 2 recto. See 24.

321. E. GUILPIN, *Skialetheia* (1598), satire 5, sig. D 6 verso. *Puisne* = young fellow.

322. THOMAS CORYAT, *Coryats crudities* (1611), sig. b 4 recto. An eccentric, Coryat (1577?–1617) won his reputation by his travels, which took him into the Middle East and even beyond, into India.

323. Sir ROBERT DALLINGTON, *A method for trauell* (1605), sig. B 1 recto. A courtier who managed to secure some minor offices, Dallington (1561–1637) was the author or translator of some works on French and Italian history.

324. Sir John Holles to the Earl of Huntingdon, February 1604 (*Historical Manuscripts Commission Report*, Portland MSS., IX (1923), 78–9).

325. William Lord Burghley, letter to his son Robert Cecil, in E. Nares, *Memoir of the life of William Cecil, Lord Burghley* (1831), III, 513. See 94.

326. 'The Surgeon's Chest': woodcut in William Clowes, *A prooued practise for all young chirurgians* (1588), p. 97 (Royal College of Surgeons). One of the most active surgeons of his time, Clowes (1540?–1614) had considerable army and navy experience, besides practising at St Bartholomew's and Christ's hospitals.

327. Surgical Instruments: woodcut in William Clowes, *A prooued practise for all young chirurgians* (1588), p. 97. See 326.

328. NICHOLAS LING, *Politeuphuia* (1598), fol. 159 recto.

329. NICHOLAS BRETON, *The good and the badde* (1616), sig. C 4 verso. See 24.

330. JOHN EARLE, *Micro-cosmographie* (1628), essay 4, sigs. B 7 verso–B 10 recto. See 149.

331. Surgical Instruments: woodcut in William Clowes, *A prooued practise for all young chirurgians* (1588), p. 97. See 326.

332. 'Claudius Holliband' (i.e. Claude Desainliens), *The Italian schoole-maister* (1597), sig. C 1 recto. See 229.

333. PHILIP STUBBES, *The second part of the anatomie of abuses* (1583), sig. H 3 recto. See 68.

334. EDWARD HAKE, *Newes out of Powles church-yarde* (1579), sig. C 5 recto. Besides being a mayor of Windsor and an M.P., Hake wrote several pamphlets castigating errors of the time.

335. *Sir William Paddy*, 1600 (St John's College, Oxford). In 1591, Paddy (1554–1634) became a Fellow of the Royal College of Physicians and later twice served as its President.

336. WILLIAM CLOWES, *A prooued practise for all young chirurgians* (1588), sigs. P 10 verso–P 11 recto. See 326.

337. JOHN DAY, *The parliament of bees*, character ix, in *Nero and other Plays*, ed. Arthur Symons (1888), p. 253. Writing mainly in collaboration, Day (c. 1574?–1640?) was another of the prolific dramatists who supplied the stage with pieces topical, satirical and poetically fantastic from the end of the century on to the reign of James.

338. 'Alchemy': title-page of Conrad Gesner, *The newe iewell of health*, translated by George Baker (1576). See 296.

339. 'An Elizabethan Laboratory': woodcut in Conrad Gesner, *The newe iewell of health*, translated by George Baker (1576), fol. 39. See 296.

340. MICHAEL DRAYTON, *Poly-Olbion* (1613), song xiii, pp. 217–18. See 35, 371.

341. 'Instrument for Distilling of the Water of Life': woodcut in Conrad Gesner, *The newe iewell of health*, translated by George Baker (1576), fol. 216. See 296.

342. *Batman vppon Bartholome* (1582), fols. 169 verso, 172 recto. A standard authority on natural philosophy from medieval times to the seventeenth century was the *De proprietatibus rerum* of Bartholomaeus Anglicus, a thirteenth-century friar. The issue of 1582 was a version of the original work with comments and additions.

343. 'Making the Instruments': woodcut in Conrad Gesner, *The newe iewell of health*, translated by George Baker (1576), fol. 115. See 296.

344. *Mary Sidney with an archlute* (Lord De L'Isle and Dudley, Penshurst Place). Mary Sidney (c. 1586–c. 1640) was the eldest daughter of Robert Sidney, Earl of Leicester: she later married Sir Robert Wroth. See 88.

345. Queen Elizabeth's virginal (Victoria and Albert Museum).

346. THOMAS DEKKER, *The double PP* (1606), sig. E 3 recto. See 5.

347. FRANCIS MERES, *Palladis tamia* (1598), p. 288. This book has won fame because of its listing of Shakespeare's plays. The author (1565–1647) was a clergyman with literary interests, evidently well acquainted with the belles lettres of his time.

348. Sir JAMES MELVILLE, *The memoires*(1683), p. 50. Melville (1535–1617) was a Scotsman who served as page to Mary Queen of Scots and who later was engaged on divers ambassadorial missions for his native country.

349. RICHARD BARNFIELD, 'To his friend Maister R. L. in praise of musique and poetrie', in 'Poems in diuers humors', added to *The encomion of Lady Pecunia* (1598), sig. E 2 recto. This poem appears also in *The passionate pilgrim*, no. 8. Barnfield (1570–1627) was a minor versifier who occasionally had flashes of higher inspiration. There are some who believe Shakespeare was the author of this sonnet.

350. JOHN DOWLAND, *The first booke of songes or ayres* (1597), dedication. One of the best of Elizabethan composers, Dowland (1563?–1626?) travelled widely and had acquaintance with many of the noted musicians of the continent.

351. WILLIAM SHAKESPEARE, *Much ado about nothing* (acted about 1598), III, iv, 39.

352. SAMUEL BIRD, *A friendly communication or dialogue betweene Paule and Demas* (1580), sig. F 2 recto and verso. The author of several theological works, Bird was minister of St Peter's, Ipswich, in the latter years of the sixteenth century.

353. 'A Consort of Musicians': detail from *Sir Henry Unton* (National Portrait Gallery).

354. *Queen Elizabeth dancing* (Lord De L'Isle and Dudley, Penshurst Place). Tradition asserts that this represents Elizabeth dancing the Lavolta. It may have been painted by Herman van der Mast (see James Laver, 'Elizabeth I and the French Dance, La Volta', *The Sphere*, 19 November 1953).

355. Sir JOHN DAVIES, *Orchestra* (1596), sigs. B 5 verso–B 6 recto. Davies (1569–1629) was an active and on the whole successful politician and statesman, holding office from 1606 to 1619 as attorney-general for Ireland. At the same time he had a decided gift for poetry: *Orchestra* and *Nosce teipsum* (1599) are among the best longer poems of the time.

356. Sir JOHN DAVIES, *ibid.* sig. B 6 recto. See 355.

357. Sir JOHN DAVIES, *ibid.* sig. B 6 verso. *Travases* = traverses. See 355.

358. Sir JOHN DAVIES, *ibid.* sig. B 6 verso. See 355.

359. Lupold von Wedel, account of visit to England, 1585, in Victor von Klarwill, *Queen Elizabeth and some Foreigners*, translated by T. H. Nash (1928), p. 338.

360. *John Bull*, 1589 (Faculty of Music, Oxford). Bull (1563–1628) was among the most famous of Elizabethan composers, and for a time was Professor of Music at Gresham's College.

361. Sir JOHN DAVIES, *Orchestra* (1596), sigs. A 5 verso–A 6 recto. See 355.

362. SAMUEL DANIEL, 'Mvsophilvs' in *The poeticall essayes* (1599), sig. F 2 recto and verso. A protégé of Lady Pembroke, Daniel (1563?–1619) gained high esteem for his sonnets to Delia (1591–2); later he turned to write a poetical *History of the Civil Wars* (1595) and the ambitious *Musophilus*. He was much interested in metrics and his *Defence of ryme*, written about 1602, is one of the important critical documents of the age. As a dramatist, he espoused the cause of the 'classical' play in *Cleopatra* (1594) and *Philotas* (1604).

363. O.B. *Qvestions of profitable and pleasant concernings* (1594), fols. 33 recto–34 recto.

364. NICHOLAS HILLIARD, self-portrait (Victoria and Albert Museum). Hilliard (1547–1619) was the most distinguished miniaturist of his time and characteristically (for 'limning' was closely asociated with the jewellers' art) he was the son of a goldsmith. In 1584 he was granted a monopoly for painting the Queen's miniature portraits.

365. *John Day*, 1562: woodcut in John Foxe, *Actes and monuments* (1563). This is the only known portrait of an Elizabethan printer or publisher. Day (1522–84) held a prominent position among the London 'stationers' of his time.

366. *Greenes vision* (1592), sig. H 1 recto.

367. Order of June 1559, in E. Cardwell, *Documentary Annals of the Reformed Church of England* (1844), I, 230. In the sixteenth century there was no copyright law, but the master-printers and publishers had a kind of control; if a book was entered in the Stationers' Register and an appropriate fee paid, action could be taken against any dishonest printer who tried to pirate it. Apart from this, the government sought to control the subject-matter of books by insisting on licence or approval of all printed matter.

368. *2 Return from Parnassus* (acted 1602), in *The three Parnassus Plays*, ed. J. B. Leishman (1949), pp. 247–8. See 129.

369. 'Presenting a Book': drawing in Sir William Teshe, *A book containing divers sorts of hands* (1580), Sloane MS. 1832, fol. 8 (British Museum).

370. *1 Return from Parnassus* (acted about 1600), in *ibid.* pp. 149–52. See 129.

371. *Michael Drayton* (National Portrait Gallery). See 35.

372. JOHN FLORIO, *A worlde of wordes* (1598), sig. a 3 verso. One of the most distinguished Italian teachers of his time, Florio (1553?–1625) is noteworthy both because of his dictionaries and of his translation of Montaigne's essays (1603).

373. WILLIAM WEBBE, *A discourse of English poetrie* (1586), sig. A 4 recto. A friend of Spenser, Webbe wrote one of the first books to be devoted to metrics and literary criticism: it is interesting that his efforts were designed to veer English verse away from native models towards classical measures.

374. *Zepheria* (1594), introductory verses, leaf following title-page.

375. *John Donne* (National Portrait Gallery). Donne's character is among the strangest of his time. All through his life (1573–1631) he was strongly urged by religious thoughts; eventually he entered the church and became Dean of St Paul's in 1621. At the same time there was a powerful sensuous quality in his being, and he first appeared as a writer with a series of satirical and other poems circulated in manuscript. These, and his later (mainly religious) writings, made him chief of the 'metaphysical' style in poetry which became fashionable in the early seventeenth century.

376. *Sir Francis Bacon* (National Portrait Gallery). Next to Shakespeare, Bacon (1561–1626) was possibly the most remarkable writer of his time—but one of totally different genius. There was not a spark of poetry in his work, and where Shakespeare stood for the antique world Bacon launched out towards the new. The era of science, alien to most Elizabethans, was clearly foreshadowed in his speculations. See 102, 250.

377. *Sir Henry Wotton*, ascribed to Sir Nathaniel Bacon, 1600 (Capt. E. G. Spencer Churchill, Northwick Park). Wotton (1568–1639) was a close friend of Donne and, like him, a poet: but he was also active in political life, starting as an adherent of Essex and later serving as ambassador abroad. ('An ambassador', he said, 'is an honest man who lies abroad for the good of his country.') Sir Nathaniel Bacon, an artist of considerable skill, was the grand-son of Sir Nicholas Bacon, the Lord Keeper.

378. MICHAEL DRAYTON, *Poems* (1619), pp. 206–7, sigs. Dd 1 verso–Dd 2 recto. It is important to realize the importance of belles lettres at the close of the sixteenth century. Shakespeare, despite the fact that many of his plays did not appear in print until 1623, was one of the most frequently printed and reprinted authors of the age; volumes of verse were issued by the dozen; and it seemed natural for many men to express themselves in poetic form. See 35, 371.

379. *William Camden*, by Marcus Gheeraerts (Bodleian Library, Oxford). There were many great scholars during the Elizabethan era, and among them not the least was William Camden (1551–1623), historian and antiquary. From 1593 to 1597 he was headmaster of Westminster School, and in 1597 he was appointed Clarenceux King-of-arms. Of his several works his *Britannia* (1586) is perhaps the most important. See 19.

380. VINCENTIO SAVIOLO, *Vincentio Saviolo his practise* (1595), sig. B 1 recto. A Paduan, Saviolo was a fencing teacher patronized by the Earl of Essex.

381. The funeral of Sir Philip Sidney, 1587; engraving by Theodor de Bry. See 22, 34, 59, 387.

382. THOMAS DEKKER, *The double PP* (1606), sig. E 3 verso. See 5.

383. Sixteenth-century close helmet (Victoria and Albert Museum).

384. HARRISON, p. 198. See 55.

385. BARNABE RICH, *A path-way to military practise* (1587), sig. G 3 recto and verso. See 113.

386. WILLIAM GARRARD, *The arte of warre* (1591), pp. 82–3. *Harquebuziers* = soldiers carrying the harquebus or arquebus, a small type of gun laid on a trestle or rest; *tire ball* = an instrument for extracting the charge: *morion* = a small helmet; *jack* = a short, tightly-fitting doublet; *curats* = cuirass; *pouldrons* = shoulder-plates; *vambraces* = armour for the arms; *tasses* = thigh-plates; *burgonet* = light helmet.

387. Helmet with porcupine crest, carried at the funeral of Sir Philip Sidney (Lord De L'Isle and Dudley, Penshurst Place). See 22, 34, 59, 381.

388. HARRISON, pp. 198–9. *Almaine* = German; *jacks* = short, tightly-fitting doublets; *fustian* = a coarse cotton material. See 55.

389. Rapier and dagger; from George Silver, *Paradoxes of defence* (1599).

390. *Sir John Sherley*, 1588. (Mrs Henry Pomeroy Davison, Sr.: photo. Frick Art Reference Library).

391. The Lord of Tyrone submitting to Sir Henry Sidney: woodcut in John Derricke, *The image of Ireland* (1581). See 99.

392. Sir JOHN SMYTHE, *Certain discourses concerning the formes and effects of diuers sorts of weapons* (1590), sigs. B 2 verso–B 3 recto. *Piquers* = pike-men; *pouldrons* = shoulder-plates; *vambraces* = armour for the arms; *tasses* = thigh-plates.

393. GEORGE SILVER, *Paradoxes of defence* (1599), sig. F 1 recto. One of the most keenly discussed questions was the relative merits of old-fashioned weapons, such as the sword, and of newer weapons, such as the rapier. At a time when muskets and pistols had come into common use and when large guns such as the culverin and basilisk could fire shot weighing from 18 to 60 pounds, there were still those who argued the merits of the old long-bow. See 389.

394. Sir JOHN SMYTHE, *Certain discourses concerning the formes and effects of diuers sorts of weapons* (1590), sig. H 3 verso.

395. *Robert Dudley, Earl of Leicester*, by Federico Zuccaro (British Museum). This is one of the only two drawings definitely known to have been executed by Federico Zuccaro during his short stay in England in 1574 and 1575. It is almost certain that the scores of pictures attributed to him have been erroneously ascribed. See 74.

396. Drill postures, armour and arms; engraving by Thomas Cookson.

397. 'The Order of March': from William Garrard, *The arte of warre* (1591), p. 92.

398. Sir John Harington, letter to his steward Thomas Combe, from Ireland, 1599, in *Nugae antiquae*, ed. Henry Harington (1804), I, 260–3. The extract refers to the ill-fated Irish expedition led by the Earl of Essex. *Kersey* = coarse woollen cloth; *Venetian* = hose of Venetian style; *Osnabridge Holland* = a kind of linen manufactured in the Netherlands and at Osnabrück; *bands* = collars, single ruffs. See 15.

399. *Henry, 5th Lord Windsor*, 1588 (Earl of Plymouth, Oakley Park). Lord Windsor (1562–1605) engaged in both the political and the military life of the time. The finely chased armour indulged in by many noblemen of the time is here well represented. Note should be taken of the emblematic background picture.

400. Inventions of War; from Thomas Smith, *Certaine additions to the booke of gvnnery* (1601).

401. Inventions of War; from Thomas Smith, *ibid.*

402. 'An Elizabethan Ship': woodcut on verso of title-page of William Bourne, *A regiment for the sea* (1574).

403. Giovanni Carlo Scaramelli, Venetian Secretary in England, report to the Doge and Senate, 20 March 1603 (*Calendar of State Papers, Venetian*, IX (1897), 557).

404. FULKE GREVILLE, *The life of the renowned Sir Philip Sidney* (1652), ed. Nowell Smith (Oxford, 1907), pp. 198–9. See 22.

405. *Sir Richard Grenville* (National Portrait Gallery). The cousin of Sir Walter Raleigh, Grenville (1541?–91) led the 1585 colonizing expedition to Virginia. After many engagements, including able service against the Armada, he met his death and won fame in the glorious fight of the *Revenge*.

406. *Sir Martin Frobisher* by Cornelis Ketel, 1577 (Bodleian Library, Oxford). Frobisher (1535?–94) is here depicted in what must be sea-dress. At the time this picture was painted he was presumably home from one of the expeditions he made between 1576 and 1578 in search of the elusive North-West Passage. Against the Armada he commanded his own ship and was knighted at sea. The painter, Cornelis Ketel, was a Dutchman who worked in England between 1573 and 1581.

407. Giovanni Carlo Scaramelli, report to the Doge and Senate, 19 February 1603 (*Calendar of State Papers, Venetian*, IX (1897), 534).

408. HARRISON, p. 163. *Kersies* = coarse woollen material; *mockadoes* = a very popular kind of cloth;

fells = skins. The original reads 'suspicious voyages'; this may be an error for 'auspicious', but (*a*) the author may be indulging in a sly hit, (*b*) he may be using 'suspicious' as though it came from the Latin *suspectus* in the sense of 'esteem'. See 55.

409. *Sir Francis Drake* (National Maritime Museum). Drake's (1540?–96) greatest exploit was his circumnavigation of the globe during the years 1577 to 1580, but all through his life he was engaged in maritime adventure and strife. In the fleet organized against the Armada he was Vice-Admiral. See 412.

410. *Phineas Pett*, by J. de Critz, 1613 (National Portrait Gallery). Particular note should be taken of the inset picture of the building of an Elizabethan galleon. Pett (1570–1647) was master-builder of the navy and was responsible for the creation of several notable ships.

411. *Sir Walter Raleigh* (National Portrait Gallery). See 37.

412. 'Drake's Dial' (National Maritime Museum). Inscribed 'Humphrey Colle made this diall anno 1569', the instrument includes (1) an armillary dial, (2) a list of latitudes of various ports, (3) a compass, (4) a list of high water tides at European harbours, (5) a perpetual calendar and (6) a means for telling the time by the Great Bear. See 409.

413. CHARLES FITZGEFFREY, *Sir Francis Drake* (1596), sig. D 4 recto. Fitzgeffrey (1575?–1638) was a clergyman who divided his time between pious works and the pursuit of poetry. *Maugre* = despite. See 409.

414. Maffio Michiel, Venetian Governor in Zante, to the Doge and Senate, 22 February 1603 (*Calendar of State Papers, Venetian*, IX (1897), 536).

415. FULKE GREVILLE, 'A treatise of monarchy', in *The Works of Fulke Greville, Lord Brooke*, ed. A. B. Grosart (1870) I, 204. See 22.

416. 'Elizabethan Shipwrights at Work': drawing in Matthew Baker, *Fragments of ancient shipwrightry* (Pepysian Library, Magdalene College, Cambridge). Baker was appointed Master Shipwright in 1572. His collection of documents relating to shipbuilding was made probably about 1586.

417. 'Draught of a Ship compared with a Fish': drawing in Matthew Baker, *ibid*.

418. 'A Map of the World': anonymous engraving, *c.* 1600. This map may be the one which was in Shakespeare's mind when he made Maria say that Malvolio smiled 'his face into more lines than are in the new map with the augmentation of the Indies'.

419. 'The English Ships arriving at Virginia': engraving by Theodor de Bry, after a drawing by John White, in Thomas Harriot, *A brief and true report of the new found land of Virginia* (Frankfurt-am-Main, 1590). A protégé of Sir Walter Raleigh and a very distinguished mathematician, Harriot (1560–1621) was an active proponent of colonization in Virginia. As an astronomer he is noteworthy for his early use of the telescope and for the observations he made on comets and sun-spots. See 37.

420. RICHARD HAKLUYT, *The principall navigations, voiages, traffiques and discoueries of the English nation* (1589) dedication. It is fitting to close these notes with a record of Hakluyt (1552?–1616), who combined in his career so many varied activities: he was an Archdeacon of Westminster, a sharer in the South Virginian Company, and the narrator-in-chief of all the many voyages undertaken by the adventurer-seamen during the sixteenth century.

421. 'Elizabeth and Fame': drawing in Sir William Teshe, *A book containing divers sorts of hands* (1589), Sloane MS. 1832, fol. 7 (British Museum).

174